Blossom

MAKING SENSE OF YOUR LIFE'S JOURNEY

Lena Edwards

TRILOGY CHRISTIAN PUBLISHERS
TUSTIN, CA

Trilogy Christian Publishers
A Wholly Owned Subsidiary of Trinity Broadcasting Network
2442 Michelle Drive
Tustin, CA 92780

Manufactured in the United States of America

10 9 8 7 6 5 4 3 2 1

Library of Congress Cataloging-in-Publication Data is available.

ISBN: 978-1-63769-602-6

E-ISBN: 978-1-63769-603-3

Contents

Dedication

I dedicate this book to all the people who helped me in my spiritual walk with God. To my mother, Sally, who has always been the rock in my family and was a dedicated prayer warrior. I also dedicate this book to my precious daughter, Sharon, who has always made me very proud. Sharon has always been an encouragement and inspiration, starting from the time she was born. I thank all the people in my life the Lord placed there for a season of encouragement. I am thankful that the Lord walked with me through many storms, which allowed me to see how awesome and powerful He is. Storms are an essential part of every good story, even in the Bible. Without my past experiences, good and bad, this book would not have been possible. The last dedication is to my brothers, Lanny Stevenson (nicknamed L. S.), who was also a poet, and John Lee, Jr. (nicknamed Duke), who was an amazing artist. Unfortunately, they both died at the young age of thirty-five, and like many others, died without ever knowing their purpose in life. Through the grace of God, Lanny gave his life to the Lord shortly before his death. I was blessed with an opportunity to talk with him for several hours before he died. I will never forget when he told me that if he were given one more chance to live, he would enjoy the simple things in life. L. S.'s last wish was that it would rain. He loved the rain, and amazingly, at the moment of his death, it started to rain. I believe God was listening to his final request. After L. S. died, I wrote the poem "When the Last Rain Drop Falls" about him. He has also inspired me to enjoy life while life is possible.

Endorsements

"It is an authentic book with non-fiction testimonies of God's miraculous powers when you trust and believe in God and His Son Jesus.

"*Blossom* is truly a must-read book; it will definitely increase your belief in God!"

—Vera Ward,
California

"When I first read my mother's book, *Blossom*, I knew it would be powerful because I had heard her poems and writings before. I never imagined that this book would give accounts of her life experiences and that poems written in this book would be just as impactful and moving as they were when I had the privilege of hearing them before they became a well-composed piece of literature. I believe these writings will be and are a blessing to everyone who reads them. It will spark a fire in people who are called to be writers to begin writing. It pricks the heart of the reader, motivating them to want to come to know Jesus."

—Sharon Ako

"Authentic is one word that Lena Edwards really embodies. She has always been an 'open book,' sharing her life experiences and lessons she has learned along the way to inspire and encourage so many. Lena is a woman of great faith and has discipled as well as been a mentor to many. Her passion for God and writing can be seen in every piece that she creates. As a creative writing teacher, Lena has made it her mission to awaken that same passion in others. Seeing her perform live on stage, I know for sure she is able to bring her words to life in a way that is energizing and inspiring."

—Robin Shannon

"We had the opportunity to teach a class together, and the topic that she taught on was confidence. The thing with teaching a topic like that is everyone knows they should be confident. So, you can't just tell people to be confident. The speaker had to inspire confidence in the listener. From the looks and responses of the audience, it was plain to see she did just that. She caused those that were listening to her to know that they could accomplish their goal and whatever it is God had called them to do. And at the same time, she commanded them to go and do it. It is a delicate balance. She did it well."

—Pastor Eldridge Ford

When the Last Raindrop Falls

His name was Lanny Stevenson, L. S. was his
nickname.
He loved laughter but hated playing games.
He was down and real; no matter what happened, L. S.
would stay the same.
He loved the rain and old-fashioned kinds of things.
His character was much like my mom's, but he looked
like dad.
I often wondered what made him so sad.
Sometimes having fun was pretending he could sing.
He never asked for much and was satisfied with just a
few things.
"I Wish It Would Rain" was his favorite tune,
Yet whenever the raindrops fell, his heart would cry
with doom.
He had many talents that surprised me: one day,
He wrote a beautiful poem about life in a special kind
of way.
But life never dealt him a fair hand,
Regardless of his problems, he tried hard to be a man.
I guess his heart was too big for this old world,
He never really looked to find that special pearl.
So he ran, he ran and never said, "I can."
He ran to a bottle called Wild Irish Rose,
He drank away his worries because life was just too
hard, I suppose.

He started manhood as early as sixteen.
He walked a rocky road, and the grass was never green.
He swallowed a lot of his anger, and his bitterness was
unseen.
I do remember one proud day: he and his buddies got
dressed up.
They were all superfly clean.
That day I saw L. S. at his best; he wasn't quite like the
others
and never tried to be like the rest.
There was something inside of him that had the poten-
tial to be the best.
But his thoughts of himself were much less.
Finally, one day when he decided to live like he should,
He found himself thinking, *If I could have only thought of
this a lot sooner,*
*But now it's too late; my body needs a new shell and
fine-tuning.*
Later, Wild Irish Rose took him away.
His family suffered a lot of sorrow and dismay.
We often said he did not have to go out this way.
If he were still here, these are the words I think he
would say:
"If you think you can't succeed, try it anyway.
Call on Jesus now,
Don't wait until your final day.
Live every moment as if it were your last.

Thank God for being the tank that feeds you spiritual
gas. You see, I made a request to God before my final
call. I asked Him if I could see my last raindrops fall. I
was blessed with time to accept Jesus in my heart,
And now, together in eternity, we will never part.
You will never see a rainbow behind a prison wall.
You will never taste infinity if sorrow makes you fall.
Relax and smell the flowers and stop crying in the rain.
Don't tease around with darkness playing deadly
games.
Live life to its fullest and answer Jesus when He calls.
Then you will find yourself smiling when your last
raindrop falls."

I love the Lord, because He has heard [and
now hears] my voice and my supplications.
Because He has inclined His ear to me, therefore will I call upon Him as long as I live. The

cords and sorrows of death were around me,
and the terrors of Sheol (the place of the dead)
had laid hold of me; I suffered anguish and
grief (trouble and sorrow). Then called I upon
the name of the Lord; O Lord, I beseech You,
save my life and deliver me!

Psalm 116:1-4 (AMPCE),
parentheses and brackets in the original

The Purpose of *Blossom*

The Spirit of the Lord GOD is upon me; because the LORD hath anointed me to preach good tidings unto the meek; he hath sent me to bind up the brokenhearted, to proclaim liberty to the captives, and the opening of the prison to them that are bound; To proclaim the acceptable year of the LORD, and the day of vengeance of our God; to comfort all that mourn.

Isaiah 61:1-2

The Bible had many writers but only one Author.

The Bible is filled with the history of Jesus the Christ, Son of the living God.

The Bible tells many stories about people who experience an encounter with Jesus, His disciples, and many other people who followed Him. Jesus is the focal point of the Bible, and He is the focus of *Spiritual Rose*.

Blossom is a spiritual writing handbook filled with testimonies of my experiences with the Lord, written in short stories in prose and poetic form.

Blossom will help anyone who desires to share his or her testimonies. It also gives exercises that will help you start your writing journey. Our stories are His story (the history of Jesus).

Revelation 12:11 says: "And they overcame him by the blood of the Lamb, and by the word of their testimony; and they loved not their lives unto the death."

Writing is a wonderful tool that can be used in many ways to spread the gospel. The gospel of Jesus Christ lives in the heart of every believer. The truth of the gospel has enabled us, believers, the privilege to experience God's power in our own lives. Our experience with God should be shared with people who do not know Him. It does not matter if we write our experiences in the form of songs, poetry, spoken word, books, or articles. It does not matter if we share it on Twitter, Facebook, email, etc., or whether we choose to tell it verbally to an audience or individuals.

Every Christian is called to be a disciple.

Writing your testimony will enable you to share it with a larger audience. People with no spiritual ears, when hearing the Word of God, may deny the Bible is truth, but they cannot deny your story. We are living testimonies for Christ, and our story is not our own. Write down your memories. Always write what God has done in your life; writing these things down will help you remember. Remembering will help build your faith. God has done many great things in my life, but it was always revealed through a need or a storm. Telling somebody your experiences with God can be written in many forms.

I Remember You

"Remember the former things, those of long ago; I am God, and there is no other; I am God, and there is none like me" (Isaiah 46:9).

I Remember You

When I was just a little girl getting my father to give me money was like fishing for diamonds in a sea filled with muddy waters. My mom warned me not to ask a stranger for money; she said, "Honey, if you ever do that again, your behind will not win." I finally looked up to the sky with the sun shining directly in my eyes and said, "God, can you give me a quarter?" I thought God wouldn't mind, and He had more than a dime. I suddenly saw a change purse a little way off, shinning in that same sun that glory was shined upon my face. I was feeling the embrace of the Father's love from above. I picked it up and opened it to see a blessing just for me. It was filled with nickels, dimes, and quarters. I remember as a child, times were rough, but my God was more than enough.

I Remember You

Being chased by many barking dogs, I could not count them all; they had four legs, I only had two. I ran out of breath, running a hole in my shoe. Suddenly, I felt as if someone lifted me up; instead of running, I felt light, as if I was flying, fearful with trembling little legs. God said, "When you could not make it through, it was I that carried you."

I Do Remember You

I remember You when my mother was dying, and I started screaming and crying, just married at nineteen. I became angry with my Lord because I was carrying the child I thought my mom would never see. I said, "If you don't save her, I will never believe." Little did I know: you can't be angry with the one you don't believe. God received even that crazy prayer.

My mother lived another thirty-six years, and our laughter dried up our tears.

I Remember You

When I was living in the fast lane like I was insane, what remained was my source of connection and protection that I knew as a child.

I use to say, "Don't leave me, I'm coming!" But the bees of death demons were swarming around me, humming.

I was in a two-car crash; I thought my life was finished.

Somehow, I came out without a scratch from the enemy's attack.

Like my shelter in a stormy rain, He came through.

Not only then but time and time again.

I Remember You

I remember my Savior was always there. I would always talk to Him in a short little prayer. "Thank You; I knew You were there. Please don't leave me. I am coming," yet the bees of darkness continued humming.

I was in debt to my neck and could not see the light for the trees.

I fell to my knees: "I beg You, Lord, please $8,000," "$13,000," then "$20,000.00," individual time. He blew my mind and paid them all; not one cent was paid by me. I give all praises to Thee. I was debt-free.

I Remember Praising You

Through my childhood years, at times, my heart would flood with tears. My dad always made me sad; the accuser made him an abuser.

When I could not take any more pain, my Savior came to my rescue.

I Remember You

He knew I was becoming depressed, and before my request, He granted me a Sabbath rest.

Christmas was the best. He made peace be still, and on the silent nights, He made me forget the wrong and remember the light that was all so pleasing and pleasantly bright. It seems as though the light destroyed darkness. He opened my eyes to see fluffy white flakes of snow like glistening confetti. As soft music played in my ears, drowning out my fears, the smell of cakes and pies my mom had baked—I could not wait. He knew just how to put back the sparkle in my eyes and make my wishes come true.

I Will Always Remember You

So many stories I can tell, so many blessings I know all so well, so many fiery furnaces I've been through, but through it all, I remembered You.

I remember Jehovah-Shammah will always be there. Our Shepherd will always care, our shelter in the rain,

Jehovah-Rapha for our pain, Jehovah-Jireh for our dept; He's the strong tower to protect us.

A shoulder for our tears, Sabbath rest for broken years, love that casts out fears. He gives us will and determination. God makes a way out of temptation. Deep calls unto deep, and we will find Him if we seek. Our good memories build our faith and love for our Lord.

Many will be overcome by the blood of the Lamb and the words of our testimonies.

Then on that final call home, God will say, "Well done, good and faithful servant, enter in I remember you."

The Ten Basic Commandents

The ten basic commandments for writing spiritual testimonies are included in this handbook. This book inspires you to tell your story to help others because your story is your ministry.

You might say, "I am not a writer," but everyone can write because writing is simply talking on paper, and this handbook can help you get started.

An example: If you could not speak because of laryngitis or any type of illness that affected your voice box, the only way you could communicate would be by writing. Writing then would become easy because it would gain purpose. You do not need to be a perfect writer to tell your story.

If you feel you do not have testimonies and have not yet experienced the goodness of Christ, then this book will be a good source that will help you know Him. When you dedicate your heart to God, you are transformed to become a child of God, and your eyes open to see He has always been with you. Starting from childhood, we were taught to write articles, essays, theses, and poetry. Writing is an essential tool for life, regardless of your occupation. When I look back at all the storms I had to face in life, I can only thank God for His grace. I realized why I had to go through so many storms. I am now honored to have the ability to share my life with others, how God has walked with me, at times carried me, and covered me through storms and the hardships that life brings.

The more I sought Him, the more inspired I became to write my life stories through poetry, songs, articles, and speaking to individuals and audiences. Many people have given their lives to Christ because of it. I've learned more about the Lord during the storms of life than during the quiet times.

This book is written in hopes that you will learn how wonderful God is, and it will inspire you to tell others how good He has been in your life. You can start by writing them down in this book.

"And we know that all things work together for good to them that love God, to them who are the called according to *his* purpose" (Romans 8:28).

God's Children Are His Garden

> I am the true vine, and my Father is the vine-dresser. Every branch in me that does not bear fruit he takes away, and every branch that does bear fruit he prunes, that it may bear more fruit.
>
> John 15:1-3

God's children are like His flower gardens.

We are all from the same God-produced family but are beautiful and divinely unique. As we transform into children of God, we blossom because the Lord's glory shines upon us. He transforms us to look like Him. We become the lights of the world. I encourage everyone to write and tell others about what the Lord has done to set you free. Your unique individual testimonies draw everyone to our Father, so they too can be adopted into the family of God.

Spiritual Rose

A rose is spiritual in every way:
It blooms in its own season.
Before it blossoms in God's sight,
The sun shines for that reason.
When it blossoms in all of its loveliness,
It's giving God the glory.
A spiritual writer is a special Rose;
Through them, God tells His story.

It shall blossom abundantly and rejoice, Even with joy and singing. The glory of Lebanon shall be given to it, The excellence of Carmel and Sharon. They shall see the glory of the LORD, The excellency of our God.

Isaiah 35:2

In Honor

In honor of my Lord and Savior, Jesus Christ, I dedicate this book. I thank Him for giving me spiritual gifts of teaching, encouraging, and helping others.

I thank Him for also giving me the talents to write and be an inspirational speaker.

These tools allow me to tell the world how He gave me life in more ways than imaginable.

One day, while surrendering my heart to the Lord in prayer, I discovered my words unexpectedly started to rhyme. After praying, I had a desire to write the prayer down. The prayer also became my promise to the Lord. This prayer was transformed into a poem called "My Prayer Today," a poem that became one of the most memorable poems I have ever written. I call it my covenant prayer to God. It was based on a desire to serve Him. God made me aware of how important the words of the poem were when He asked that I tell somebody!

I placed it on the wall of my prayer room. Every day, I live this promise in faith and hope, drawing closer to Him and abiding in His love. I meant every word with all of my heart. I never knew how much I had to grow to fully understand the depth of my own promise to Him in this poem until my life started to reflect it through my storms. My trials and triumphs have taken me from faith to faith and glory to glory. I am still living it out and will continue until His return.

Prayer Today

I need You, Lord, to rescue me.
"Please hold on to Me and I to you,"
This is what You told me to do.
I will be Your token,
I will be Your godly spoken.
I will be Your mouth for others to hear,
I'll be Your light for others to see,

I'll be You, the Spirit in me.
I'll be a flower with mighty power.
So please, hold my hand,
And for You, I'll stand on a rock of salvation
For the entire nation to see You in me.
Please deliver the Spirit in me,
Spread my wings and set me free
So I could fly the highest high.
For You, I'll die if You rely on me,
I give You my life that You own anyway.
This is the prayer I pray today.

Purpose for Testimonies

They overcame him by the blood of the Lamb and by the word of their testimony; they did not love their lives so much as to shrink from death. Therefore rejoice, you heavens and you who dwell in them! But woe to the earth and the sea, because the devil has gone down to you! He is filled with fury, because he knows that his time is short.

Revelation 12:10-12 (NIV)

Spiritual testimonies are birthed out of the tests we have faced through life from time to time, tests that God allows that we may come to know Him. When we come to the revelation of who God is, our testimony becomes that powerful story that brings others to know Him.

Sharing is also healing for the messenger. As you write down your story and hear with your own ears what God has done for you, it helps you to remember God's love, power, and grace. We are called by God to be fishers of men. We survived in order to help unbelievers to know God. We are the lights of this dark world. By sharing our testimonies, we are sharing the awesome power and love of God.

The Unexpected Visit in 1974

I was newly married, pregnant, and twenty years old during the year 1974. One day, I had an unexpected visit from my parents. My parents knocked on the door of my small apartment, and my father walked in with a very sad, bizarre look on his face. My parents came to let me know the worst news I had ever heard in the twenty years of my life. They told me they had been to the doctor's office, and my mother had three months to live. I was shocked and speechless.

A few years prior to hearing this bad news from my parents, my mother delivered her last child, my little sister, Ann. Ann was also her tenth child. The doctors told her she could no longer have any more children because of some serious complications during delivery. Due to the complications, the doctor performed a hysterectomy. Because of this, she no longer had menstrual cycles. Unexpectedly, a few years later, she started hemorrhaging while on vacation with my father and two younger siblings. She never thought she was actually hemorrhaging because she was not experiencing any pain at all.

She thought it was not that serious, and they both believed it might be another menstrual cycle. She was always energetic and would exercise regularly. One day, while exercising, she felt more tired than usual. She later started to become more fatigued and was unable to exercise at all. She then realized her condition might be serious, so she made an appointment to see a doctor. During her doctor's visit, she had to have several X-rays of her abdomen.

The doctor discovered something unusual on the X-rays that looked like small cancerous tumors. The doctor decided to operate to remove them, but the surgery was unsuccessful. He tried a second time to remedy the problem and not only failed again but discovered the cancer was rapidly spreading. After the doctor's unsuccessful attempts to remove the cancer, they sent my mother home and proclaimed there was nothing else they could do. Over a short period of time, the cancer spread over most of her body.

My parents' visit to the doctor to hear the verdict on that day was the same day of their unexpected visit to my home. The doctor's final diagnosis was the worst.

My mother had only three months to live. That day, I became so afraid I refused to believe it. I thought, *How could this be?* I was angry and in shock. My oldest brother, Earnest, called me later to help me deal with the bad news. My brother had been to Vietnam and was emotionally stronger than I. I became even angrier when he tried to make me face what was going to happen to my mother, but somehow I could not receive this bad news.

Later that night, I got on my knees and started arguing with God. I was angry with God and disappointed when I realized I had never really gotten the chance to know my mother more personally. Being raised in a family of ten made it hard for me to spend quality time with her. I prayed even though I was not living a devoted Christian life. I knew God existed through my mother. I gave Him my heart at church and was baptized when I was thirteen years old, but I did not understand what it all meant. I remember I used to walk past my parents' bedroom to go to the bathroom before going to bed. The door would always be open, and I would see my mother on her knees, praying. She was the only one in my family who was truly living as a Christian. I did not ask God but told Him out of ignorance, "If You allow my mother to die, I will never believe in You!" I asked Him to allow her to live so that she could see the birth of my own child. I asked Him to allow her to live long enough for us to develop a personal mother-daughter relationship.

Later that night, I had a dream. I attended a funeral, and strangely, my mother was seated right next to me. I did not know who was in the casket. God told me my mother would not die. He told me in the dream to go over to her house and lay my hands on her and pray for her. I prayed when I was a little girl, but I thought praying for someone who was sick was much more complicated. But God's voice was like a record, repeating in my head over and over, "Go over and pray for your mother."

I lived 4500 North in Chicago at the time, and my parents lived 2500 West in Chicago. I did not have a car at the time, so I took the bus. I was fearful yet hopeful that God would heal her. I thought, *I heard from God, or I am completely going insane.*

My mother was lying in her bed. She had lost a tremendous amount of weight, and she was wearing a colostomy bag because she was no longer able to go to the bathroom on her own. I came over and talked with my two younger siblings, Ann and Joyce; they were about five and nine years of age. I asked them to come with me and pray for Mom. I laid my hands on her wound, and we prayed. After I came out of the room, a sense of peace came over me.

Two or three weeks later, my mother went back to her doctor for a checkup, and the doctor gave her another X-ray. After looking over the X-ray, they did not see any signs of cancer. They later took another X-ray: still no signs of cancer. The doctor finally concluded the cancer was in remission. Later they gave her other X-ray tests, and still the same diagnosis. I knew God had healed my mother. Some people were doubtful, and they thought her healing was only temporary. I knew the Lord completely healed her.

My mother was blessed to live thirty-six more wonderful years. At the age of eighty-one, she was still driving and working in the church. We've had wonderful personal days together; she was there when my daughter was born, she lived to see her get married. My siblings and I learned to appreciate her more as we grew as adults. She became my best friend and confidant. I called her almost every day and let her know I love her. I've learned so much about my mother from the time she was a little child through her adulthood, and I am grateful I learned some valuable life lessons and about Jesus. Her church gave her an honorary service one year before she was translated to God's kingdom. Most of my family attended the service; we gave her honor. We had no idea she would be going home the following year. She was an intercessor for our family. Many of my siblings and I are now living Christian lives. For her going home service, each of my siblings gave me their personal experiences to write in verse. Praise God to the highest!

What the Enemy Tries to Stop, God's Grace Makes Happen

One day while picking up a few items from a grocery store, I was standing in line, waiting to be checked out by the cashier, when suddenly, a grocery cart came charging into me. A lady purposely pushed her cart to hit me with it. She then looked at me as if I committed a crime against her. I could not figure out what I had done to make her so angry. I did not see her until I stepped in line. There was a man behind me and another man in front of me, and she was with the person in front of me. It seemed as though she walked out of the line with her cart and came back. I noticed she was trying to get in front of me to be reunited with the man in front of me to finish checking out. Before I could step back a few inches to let her back in line, she pushed her cart and hit me. She never apologized but only glanced at me with an evil look.

I had no idea at the time why she attacked me, but I got very angry. I almost had a strong desire to push my cart into her. I thank God for the Holy Spirit, who helped me to control my emotions. He used a man who stood behind me, who watched the entire incident.

Suddenly he spoke out and said, "Do not respond to her, just simply ignore her." He said it twice. When I looked at him, I knew this was coming from the Lord, so I stood, angrily yet silently, waiting until my turn to check out. After checking out, I quickly left the store before I allowed the anger to fester. As hard as it was while waiting, I did not retaliate.

Everything within me wanted to argue. I felt it was unjust. I realized it was an attack from the enemy. At that moment, I started to see things from a spiritual perspective. I felt somehow this was a test, or God was about to do something. I was angry and confused until a few minutes later. After exiting the store, while walking back to my car, a young lady sitting in a parked car called out to me, "Excuse me, miss!" I looked around, and she was sitting on the passenger side in a car with the windows down. She said, "I am sorry to bother you, but I would like to know where you got your hair done. I love it!" I was a little skeptical at first, but I stopped anyway. I stood a few feet away and looked into the back seat to make sure no one else was in the car.

I wanted to make sure it was not a scam or trick. After realizing she was alone, I replied, "Thank you! I don't have the shop's information with me, but if you give me your number or email, I could give it to you when I get home." I thought, *I can't believe she likes my hair. It's time to go back to the shop.* I thought this morning it was looking pretty bad. At that moment, the incident in the store did not seem as important. I began to smile. We started talking about various hairstyles, which led to more conversation about other things.

I began to think that this might be a purpose-driven meeting. The Lord started to download information into my head. He gave me a lot of personal information about her. There have been many times that God would give me personal information about a person to get their attention so that I could be a witness for Him. I began to ask her questions based on what the Lord had given me. I made statements about her personal life that shocked her. After I had gotten her undivided attention, I started to testify about the Lord. She asked me how I knew so much about her. She even asked me if I was an angel.

I told her that the Lord told me about her to get her attention, and I also told her how much He loved her. I spoke to her about forgiveness. God wanted her to forgive a family member who hurt her. He wanted to save her from the unhappy life she was currently living. After our conversation, I knew her heart was open and ready to receive Christ. I asked her if she wanted to give her heart to the Lord, and I told her I would pray for her. She said, "Yes." I asked her to repeat after me the words to salvation. She confessed Jesus was the Lord, repented for her sins, and asked Him to come into her heart. After her confession, we held hands as I prayed for her. She began to cry tears of joy. God had already gone before me and prepared her heart. After I prayed for her, I gave her the address of my church.

She came the following Sunday. When I saw her, I came up to greet her, and she said to me, "I came here because I wanted to come to the church, but I also wanted to see if you were an angel or human. Because there is no way you would have known so much about me unless God told you."

At times, the devil knows that God is getting ready to use us, so we must always try to be aware of his attacks. I almost lost, but God sent someone to calm me. It was my decision to choose the right thing to do. I am glad I listened to the spirit of God instead of my flesh. God's grace is so amazing. He used a stranger to speak to me. The enemy tried his best to stop it, but God still made it happen.

God will do whatever is necessary to save souls, even if it means downloading details of someone's life into our mind to capture their attention for salvation.

Having the love and passion for others is *Emmanuel* ("God in us"). He gives us supernatural abilities by putting His super divinity within our mortal bodies to be His disciples. How powerful is that!

"And God said, Let us make man in our image, after our likeness" (Genesis 1:26).

How to Produce Fruit

The poem I wrote below, titled "Producing Fruit," was written to encourage Christians to be disciples. It is not for us to only be disciples outside the walls of our church but also on the inside. There may be someone new in your church or workplace who needs to be validated. They need to know that someone cares. We need to always be spiritually aware of our surroundings to win souls for the Lord.

Producing Fruit

She always sat in the last row; she carried a look of
despair.
A heavy burden was deep within because her eyes
would
take me there.
When I walked over to greet another, I recognized
the expression on her face,

An expression that was hardened by anger, a look that
was
hard to embrace.
When she glanced at me, I heard an invitation, calling
me to
be a friend.
It was the Holy Spirit prompting me to make the first
move
and enter in.
But I walked away with my mindset not to return
again,
The coldness of her spirit and my fear of battling with
sin.
But a thought crossed my mind like a sailboat floating
against the wind,
"You are My disciple, and I have created you to be
fishers
of men."
I knew I had to talk to her regardless of fear or what
she
might say.
I had to embrace her with love, so I asked the Holy
Spirit to
show me the way.
The next week, I was determined to speak whenever
the
service would end.

My flesh was at war with my spirit; it looked impossible for

me to win.

Then a voice cried out, "I can do all things through
Christ

who strengthens me."

Had I forgotten I was once blind, and someone prayed
that I

might be set free?

I'll do it!

And I will get through it.

And I will stick to it.

"Hello, my name is Roslyn; I don't think I've met you
before.

It's so nice to see you; can I get you a visitor's
brochure?"

"No, I have one; you may think that I'm a visitor because I

don't come every week?

But I've come enough to see you; I remember you always sit in the same seat."

"Fifth row, number three, that's me; I've been here for
seven years.

In that seat, I've shouted, sung songs, and shed many
joyful tears.

By the way, would you like to go for dessert and coffee,
I

know of a wonderful café?"

"Yes, I don't mind," she replied, "but I have no money.
Are you
going to pay?"

"Sure, it's my treat; we can get to know each other and
discuss the message of today."

As we entered the café, I noticed her coat was old,
worn, and ripped,

Her shoes had walked their last mile, and her purse
had a
broken zip.

She said the menu looked good, "I'm starved; I don't
know if I want lunch or sweets."

"The sky is the limit," I smiled and quietly replied, "pick
as
much as you desire to eat."

I said, "I know you don't know me well, but I would like
to
buy you a new coat."

She looked quite surprised and said, "Are you kidding
me,
Is this a joke?"

I said, "If I offended you, please forgive me; I'll never
ask again."

"Oh no!" she replied with tears in her eyes; I just realized God
sent me a friend.

She said, "I've been attending this church for a while,
but no
one noticed me but you."
I looked into her eyes and realized I was seeing her
now with
a different point of view.
As time rolled on, our fellowship was made strong
through
God's wisdom, love, and grace.
When the season was over like a four-leaf clover,
She was picked out to take others to a higher place.
I ate at the same café one sunny day and saw her
witnessing
to a little girl and her mother.
As she testified, teardrops fell from my eyes; I realized
she
was now mentoring another.
Disciples are leaders from Christ to reproduce fruit;
He
made us to be fishers of men.
We are the head and not the tail to conquer and pre-
vail, to
be bold enough to win.

Writing exercise number one. Pretend someone is asking you this question: "What has God done for you that you know He did without doubt?" What would you say?

_____

_____

_____

_____

_____

_____

_____

_____

_____

_____

_____

_____

_____

_____

_____

_____

_____

What Are Poetic Testimonies?

Poetry is rhythmic words that flow much like various styles of music. Poetry can be written in a short or long form, quotes or parables, repetitious or abstract. Poetry does not always rhyme, nor does it need to; it all depends on the poet and the styles he or she chooses to write in. There are many types of poems that are written in many styles.

Your testimony can be written as a poem, like many poems that I share in this book. Spiritual poetry is a gift from God that has been overlooked for years in some churches. Spiritual poetry has not been taken as seriously as music.

There are five books of spiritual poetry in the Bible: Job, Psalms, Proverbs, Ecclesiastes, and the Song of Solomon. The book of Psalms is a good illustration of poetic spiritual testimonies and prayers.

My two personal favorites are Psalms and the Song of Solomon.

David, king of Israel, wrote many of the chapters in the book of Psalms. The book of Psalms reveals many prayers and experiences of David, written in poetic form. The poems speak about his frustrations, pains, and anger, as well as his remarkable joys, gladness, and peace. He shares many of his trials and triumphs in poetic testimonies written for us to understand our feelings as Christians. They also teach us how to share them with the Lord.

Below is an example of a poem from the book of Psalms.

> Lord, how are they increased that trouble me! Many are they that rise up against me. Many there be which say of my soul, There is no help for him in God. Selah.
> But thou, O LORD, art a shield for me; my glory, and the lifter up of mine head. I cried unto the LORD with my voice and he heard me out of his holy hill. Selah. I laid me down and slept; I awaked; for the LORD sustained me.
> I will not be afraid of ten thousands of people, which have set themselves against me round about. Arise, LORD; save me, O my God: for thou hast smitten all mine enemies upon the

cheek bone; thou hast broken the teeth of the ungodly. Salvation belongeth unto the LORD: thy blessing is upon thy people. Selah.

Psalm 3

The Song of Solomon: Solomon is the son of David, who became king after the death of his father. He wrote the Song of Solomon. It consists of love letters or sonnets expressing God's love for man. It shares chapters that express the deep love between a married man and woman so that we can have a glimpse of understanding how much God loves us. Solomon experienced love from God and love from man. He expressed it in his poetic testimonies.

Below is an example of a poem from the Song of Solomon.

Place me like a seal over your heart, like a seal on your arm; for love is as strong as death, its jealousy unyielding as the grave. It burns like blazing fire, like a mighty flame. Many waters cannot quench love; rivers cannot wash it away. If one were to give all the wealth of his house for love, it would be utterly scorned.

Song of Solomon 8:6-7 (NIV)

The book of Job is a poetic story about the pain a man suffered spiritually, mentally, and physically, all at the same time. It teaches us how friends can completely turn on you during times of need. It teaches how weak we really are without the Lord and how much pain a man can endure when he is spiritually mature and still loves and trusts the Lord. Yet it is a testimony about Job's triumph, how he passed the test of suffering that was ordered by God and then was blessed by God and increased even more spiritually.

"Though he slay me, yet will I trust in him: but I will maintain mine own ways before him" (Job 13:15).

God puts messages in poems, which become crystal clear yet can remain a mystery. When God gets ready to unveil the mysteries of spiritual parables, metaphors, or hidden messages of revelation, He opens the spiritual ears of those who need to hear them for application in their life. Then the message is crystal clear.

"He who has ears to hear, let him be listening and let him consider and perceive and comprehend by hearing" (Matthew 11:15, AMPCE).

I used to go to many cafés that had an open-mic night for poets, singers, and musicians, artists who wanted to share their talents with an open audience. Many people would share their personal stories through poetry and songs; even the sound of instrumental music would let you know what they have gone through in life. They were eager to express and share their personal stories with total strangers by way of the arts. Some artists who were sharing other than believer's poems were very depressing. They would often talk about their pain and heartaches that would leave many people hanging, wondering if they had ever been healed from their pain. At times, I would hear the bitterness and anger expressed in their work, yet unresolved or with no solution for the issues they faced. There was one difference between the people who believed in Christ and the nonbelievers. Some believers seemed to have the answers to the heartaches in their lives. They would often recite poems about their problems and then talk about how the Lord brought them out of it, much like biblical poetry. I found how wonderful it was to actually recite a poem that expressed how God had saved me from a bad situation.

I was happy to share the wonderful powers and wisdom of the Lord and how much He loved us, and oftentimes, I would look at the audience and see expressions of wonder and amazement. Cafés and poetry venues were my outlets to witness poetically.

Later, I started to share a poem anywhere if given the opportunity because some people would rather listen to a poem than listen to words from the Bible. Witnessing to others about the Lord can be done in various ways.

A Victim of Abuse

I grew up in a large family: nine siblings and two parents.

My mother got married at seventeen, and my father was twenty. My father was abused as a child. I learned very early in life that hurting people hurt people. My father became very angry and bitter, starting when I was only six or seven years of age. He was always angry for no reason. I remember my siblings and I used to wish he did not come home from work. My sister described him as an angry lion. We received many unjust beatings, and we were yelled at continuously almost every day. I will never forget getting the worst beating while I was still sleeping. My father beat me while sleeping because he said I did not wake up to get dressed for school when he called me. I do not need to go any further with this story because it is a book alone.

Needless to say, I wanted to leave home so badly that I considered joining the army. Instead of joining the army, I got married at nineteen. I thought I was getting away from an angry lion, and I married one. I got married to another abuser. I went from the skillet to the frying pan.

I did not realize that my mother was also a victim of my father until I got married. I understood the fear of being married to someone who was angry. From this point, my life seemed to head on a downhill slope. I did not feel worthy of love; I thought no one loved me.

It was even hard for me to love myself. "Red Pointed Arrows" is my testimony written in poetic form. This is also an example of a poetic testimony when God turned my world around by walking directly into one of the worst storms of my life.

Red Pointed Arrows

I was introduced to someone called Anger
when I was just a child.
It was a curse from someone that hurt me
when my mind was free and wild.
When Anger met Pain, they moved into my heart.
As I grew older, Insecurity played its part.
Insecurity was introduced to Lonely,
and together, they were friends.
They played a game with Sadness,
and Desperation moved right in.
Desperation came with Impatience,

and they brought with them a revolving door.
Many came to meet my heart
so that Lonely would cry no more.
As the revolving door spun and turned,
many came in and left out.
They brought with them so much Hurt,
my heart would scream, "Get out!"
The rocks from spoken words cover my heart with a
shield,
The shield was made of Sorrow and Sadness,
so my tears turned into steel.
Lonely, Sorrow, and Sadness were so well covered
they buried their name,
But Bitter, Hatred, and Anger hardened
and stayed the same.
They all got together and painted a picture of fire red.
Red pointed arrows started to shoot bullets

A ball of Confusion came knocking at my door,
It gave me a death delusion so that I may live no more.
Painted red drew a knife and placed it in my hand,
Then I heard the tracking of footsteps
walking swiftly through the sand.
A sudden wind blew in a whisper
that spoke love into my ear.
There was trouble all around me,
but strangely, there was no fear.
As this hand reached out to grab me,
it tossed away my knife
The arrows ceased, the bullets stopped,
Anger and Bitter ran away with strife.
The steel from my eyes was melted into tears.
Desperation and Lonely were well-forgotten
when Security appeared.
My spirit was reborn; to my life were added years.
He washed away the dirt and dried up all my tears.
He sent crystal pastel colors and wiped away the red.
This power gave me the highest high
that spun inside my head.
The magnifying power and glory
blew Confusion from my mind.
I needed to check Delusion, so I spent some praying
time.
My heart overflowed like a deep, wide, clear river.
"Hallelujah!" My mouth yelled out

as I was being delivered.
I started a journey seeking to find Him;
I needed to know His name.
Suddenly, from a cloud, a whispered, "Jesus...Jesus..."
My life has never been the same.
Now, when red pointed arrows dare to shoot bullets,
and I'm in need of protection;
I call on the name of Jesus,
And the arrows flee in seven different directions.

We must pray for wisdom and guidance for our steps to be ordered by the Lord. He can turn a bad situation into a blessing. Experiences become testimonies helping others by letting them know how God brought you through. This can encourage others to trust in God.

For we do not have a High Priest who is unable to understand and sympathize and have a shared feeling with our weaknesses and infirmities and liability to the assault of temptation. But one who has been tempted in every respect as we are. Yet without sin.

Hebrews 4:15 (NIV)

Ten Basic Commandments for Spiritual Writing

If we are going to be influenced by God to write in the spirit, there are ten commandments to follow:

First Commandment: Give Your Heart to God

Spiritual conversion is essential to writing spiritually. There is an extra measure of responsibility for writing when writing for God's glory. Writing your story to testify about Him is a form of worship. It requires integrity, honesty, and truth. The Bible says in John 4:24, "God is a Spirit and they that worship Him must worship Him in spirit and in truth." Seek to know God through prayer, reading His Word, spending alone time with Him, and fellowshipping with other believers.

Spiritual development and growth will help conquer fear and release the spiritual writer in you.

"For God so loved the world, that he gave his only begotten Son, that whosoever believeth in him should not perish, but have everlasting life" (John 3:16).

Second Commandment: Have Faith

"So then faith cometh by hearing, and hearing by the word of God" (Romans 10:17).

We are all given a measure of faith when we first believe. God lives in us, and He has already given us the ability to communicate in writing. Writing is speaking on paper. There will be times when God will speak and tell you specifically what to write. He has already prepared an audience for you where hearts are open and ready to hear your story. There will also be times when He will not speak. That should not stop you from writing your testimony and sharing it with others.

We do not always need to be tapped on the shoulder to tell others of His good news. When you believe, as you share your testimony, others will believe also.

We should have enough faith to know that our testimonies will not go in vain.

If God leads you to talk to someone, do it and leave the rest up to Him. Know that our messes are converted to powerful messages when we are delivered and become children of Christ. "Faith without works is dead" (James 2:20). If He gave you a story, it is for His glory.

Third Commandment: Never Miss the Mark

"The soul of the sluggard craves and gets nothing, while the soul of the diligent is richly supplied" (Proverbs 13:4, ESV).

Have you ever had a spontaneous moment when you felt like doing something but waited too long and lost the desire? There are moments God sets the tone for writing. If you acknowledge those moments by stopping whatever you are doing and writing down those thoughts, you will suddenly know exactly what to write about. You may finish it at that moment, or you may finish it later.

Don't become lazy; if you miss the mark, it will never come in that tone again.

Writing down the initial thought that comes at that moment is an important factor in writing. I have been asked to write personal poems for weddings, funerals, family reunions, birthdays, etc. Many people were joyfully amazed by the knowledge I had of their personal lives, but God gave me the knowledge when He set the tone. If I did not write it down, I would have missed the mark. Regardless of the purpose when the tone is set, write the thought down immediately.

Fourth Commandment: Your Heart Is the First Heart Your Message Should Touch

"A man shall eat good by the fruit of his mouth: but the soul of the transgressors shall eat violence" (Proverbs 13:2).

Be sure that whatever you write ministers to you first. After it excites you or ministers to you, then read it again to someone else. Many times while reading your work to another individual, it enables you to hear it clearly. Spiritual writing comes from the heart and ministers to hearts that are listening. Did it touch you?

Fifth Commandment: Stay True to Self

"And ye shall know the truth, and the truth shall make you free" (John 8:32).

It is very important to be yourself. Truth sets people free. God calls us out to be different from the world, and at times, it is not easy because the world is filled with carbon copies, people trying to be like other people. When we are true to ourselves, it honors God.

God created everyone to be uniquely different. We are like a garden of flowers, and God is the keeper of the garden. Even though the flowers drink from the same water, grow from the same dirt, and blossom from the same sunlight, their overall appearance is completely different. We live different lives, we all express our emotions and feelings differently, and we see life differently. There are some people who will understand God through your story alone.

Sixth Commandment: Never Write Frustrated

"For the anger of man does not produce the righteousness of God" (James 1:20, ESV).

If you are struggling or feel frustrated, put the pen down and pray. Wait until you can calm your spirit and think clearly. We cannot restore or encourage from a spirit of anger or frustration. Whatever you are feeling will reflect in your writing. Even if you are only sending an email, the reader will know if you are angry. If you are not flowing, it is not the right time to write. Spiritual writing does not require brainstorming because God is all wisdom and all knowledge, and He lives in us. Moreover, He is the "Prince of Peace." His peace does not allow frustration.

Seventh Commandment: Help Tools Are Necessary

"Iron sharpeneth iron; so a man sharpeneth the countenance of his friend" (Proverbs 27:17).

Know that we all can make a mistake, which is why God has given some people the talent to create help tools. Have at hand a dictionary, thesaurus, and rhyming dictionary. These tools are helpful for better writing. Many help tools are on your computer as well. Another means for help is to have someone you trust to edit your work; some people are very good at editing.

There will be words that may be grammatically correct but may not flow right with your message. Finding a different word with the same meaning may sound better with your message. Finding the best words is like finding that perfect pair of shoes or tie that fits an outfit worn on a special occasion. Learning to use help tools not only sharpens what you write but also sharpens you as a writer.

Eighth Commandment: Stay Humble

"Humble yourselves, therefore, under the mighty hand of God so that at the proper time he may exalt you" (1 Peter 5:6, ESV).

"Pride goes before destruction, a haughty spirit before a fall" (Proverbs 16:18, NIV).

Stay humble at all times, never become boastful or prideful. God hates pride.

We should only be boastful about God's goodness in our lives. Consider it a blessing that He has chosen us to talk about our relationship with Him. God hates when we glorify self by giving ourselves glory. He is also a jealous God. The humble understand God's grace and know they are spiritually bankrupt without Him. They recognize their desperate need for Him at all times.

"Blessed are the pure in heart: for they shall see God" (Matthew 5:8).

Ninth Commandment: Have a Plan

"The soul of the sluggard craves and gets nothing, while the soul of the diligent is richly supplied" (Proverb 13:4, ESV).

Your storms have a purpose, so always develop a plan where you will market or display your work. Spend time in prayer by asking God to lead you to the proper place for your work to be read or on display. We must always keep in mind why we are writing: to help others. Someone somewhere is going through what you have already endured, and they need to know how you made it through. It cannot get to them without God's plan.

Tenth Commandment: Stay Focused

"A double-minded man is unstable in all his ways" (James 1:8).

"A person who has doubts is thinking about two different things at the same time and can't make up his mind about anything" (James 1:8, GW).

Jumping from one subject to the next weakens the message. Stick to the point; when writing, try not to stray too far from the general message.

Write Your First Experience with God

Testimonies should start with your experiences leading up to your relationship with God. What happened that caused you to cry out to God? How has your life changed since your conversion?

"And they overcame him by the blood of the Lamb, and by the word of their testimony; and they loved not their lives unto the death" (Revelation 12:11).

Optional: write down the scripture or scriptures that best describes your situation.

Write on this page your first experience with God. Be sure to include the answers to the questions asked above when writing your first testimony.

_____

_____

_____

_____

_____

_____

_____

_____

_____

_____

Toothache and Car Problems Testimony

It was the year 2000. During the late evening hours, I was relaxing in my apartment on the north side of Chicago when a couple of Chicago police officers raced down the street where I lived during a police chase. Later I heard a very hard knock at my door. It was a Chicago policeman coming to inform me they hit my car that was parked in front of my apartment. They also wanted to give me a number to call the next day to report the damages to my car.

After looking at the damages, I noticed the way the car was hit on the side caused the dent to push into the tire, making it difficult for me to drive. The police stated that it would not be a problem; the City of Chicago would take care of it. The following day I called the number they gave me for repairs. The insurance representative stated that it would be at least a year before they could fix my car. They also stated I would need to mail them three estimates from different auto repair shops. I was very angry about the length of time it would take for them to repair my car, plus the time and inconvenience it would take just getting the estimates. To add to the auto problems, my tooth started to ache like never before. I could expect a headache, but a toothache? As time passed, the pain worsened. The toothache pain got so bad I could not bear it.

I ran into my bedroom, fell on the bed in serious pain, and started crying out to God. My credit card was full, and the credit card company would not allow me to put another penny on my card without paying for the large debt I had already accumulated on the card.

I did not make much money at my job at the time and did not have dental insurance. I thought, *What could be worse? A car I cannot drive, plus a toothache I cannot bear.* I pleaded with the Lord to help me. A few minutes later, I heard the Lord speak to my heart very loudly and clearly: "Where is your faith?"

Suddenly, fear came over me. Then I heard Minister Joyce Meyer's voice: "If you are afraid, do it in fear." I realized I needed to get painkillers to stop the pain and then find a dentist close by. I suddenly remembered a coworker mention in a brief conversation a good dentist whose office was located downtown. He gave me his business card. I rubbed some toothache medication on my gums to stop the pain and headed downtown on the train to the dental office.

I was not as concerned about my car until I got rid of the toothache. The dentist took care of emergency patients right away. The wait was only fifteen minutes. The dentist was nice and explained what he needed to do. The receptionist came into the room to take a dental insurance card or a credit card. Needless to say, by faith, I gave her my credit card, hoping she would not come back to tell me it had been declined. She ran the credit card while the dentist deadened my mouth so there would not be any pain. The dentist completed the work in one hour. I headed to the receptionist to take care of the bill. I found out the credit card went through. I was happy the pain was gone and the credit card went through without any problems, by the grace of God. The charge was $800.

Later, after going home, I took a second look at my car. A thought came to mind: *If the credit card went through okay for the dentist, maybe I could try again for the car repairs. I could fix it right away and send the bill to the City of Chicago for reimbursement.*

I called the City the next day to get authorization to repair my car right away at a shop near my home. The City allowed it, so I took my car into a shop two blocks away to keep from driving it too far with the damages.

God allowed another $350 credit for the car repair to go through as well. Even though I was grateful, I thought maybe God would give me some money somehow to take care of the credit card bills. One month later, I received my credit card bill. I looked at the statement detail, and to my surprise, it said, "Thank you for the $800 payment." On the next line, it said, "Thank you for the $350 payment." I rubbed my eyes and looked at the statement again. I could not believe it.

I called my friend, who was also a Christian. I was excited and filled with joy. After telling her my good news, her response surprised me. She said, "They may have made a mistake, and they will find it later on." I was so upset with her response because she did not believe it was God, even though I told her and she was a Christian. I immediately hung up the phone. I did not want to talk to her about it anymore. In fact, I was afraid to call anyone because I thought they would rob me of my joy.

God paid the bills, and it has been ten years since the incident, yet the credit card company never sent a notice of correction. I know, without a doubt, it was the Lord. How bizarre. Both payments were paid in the exact amount that was charged. Needless to say, my faith increased even more. One thing I will always remember in the Bible: "God is our refuge and strength, a very present help in trouble" (Psalm 46:1).

Contract with Man versus Covenant with God

A contract is different from a covenant. A contract is a binding agreement between two or more persons that is enforceable by law and can be broken if one of the parties of the contract does not honor the terms of the contract. Man's contracts are subject to failure.

But God's covenant with us is His sure promise. What can be surer than God, who sent His only Son to die for us to ensure His promises are true?

> But now hath he obtained a more excellent ministry, by how much also he is the mediator of a better covenant, which was established upon better promises. For if that first covenant had been faultless, then should no place have been sought for the second. For

finding fault with them, he saith, Behold, the days come, saith the Lord, when I will make a new covenant with the house of Israel and with the house of Judah.

Hebrews 8:6-8

God made many promises to me and kept all of them. One of the promises was that my daughter would be married. I always wanted my daughter to be married. She, too, wanted to be married, but she was not seeking a husband; she was seeking God. I prayed for God to send her a husband.

One night I had a dream: I saw a man whose face I could not clearly see. He was cooking and staring at my daughter, who was also cooking. My daughter is an executive chef, so it was not unusual that she would be cooking in my dream. When I woke up, I explained to my daughter that she needed to start praying for her husband. I told her to write down what she wanted from him. I knew from the dream this man lived on the south side of Chicago. I also knew he was going to meet her in one year.

In one year, she met him, and it was love at first sight. He was everything she asked for. God answered my prayer. In a dream, He promised me it would happen, and it did. I can now testify that when God makes a promise, it will come true because God's promise, like

His covenant, is truth, and truth sets anyone free of doubt.

Do you remember a promise God made to you, and you were excited when He fulfilled it? Write on the spaces below a promise that can also become a testimony to tell someone that God's promises are real in your life.

_____

_____

_____

_____

_____

_____

_____

_____

_____

_____

_____

_____

_____

_____

_____

_____

_____

_____

_____

Covenant with Jesus

As we climb up the down staircases of life
and each step seems too hard to bear,
When we come to the end of our ropes,
and there is very little hope to spare,
When we are down to our last dime,
and life seems so unfair,
Remember: we have a covenant with God.
Endorsed with Jesus's blood,
It's certified and approved,
It's guaranteed with His agape love.
We were picked out and set aside for His purpose and
plan.
We are the chosen generation, a royal priesthood,
We are the rocks that must and will stand.

We are molded in the fire and polished to shine
like God's Son.
We are the end-time generation, empowered before
life
on the earth had begun.
We need not be pressed down with hardship and
despair—
The blood covenant is God's blessed assurance
that He cares.
Pain may endure for a night, but joy will certainly
blossom
in the morning.
As surely as the sun will rise, latter rain will release
a fresh dawning.
Application of His Word empowers us with hope
for great expectations,
So we resist temptation through knowledge
by understanding our identification.
At the fullness of time, He will release the
manifestation
Of His powerful revelation through us to increase
the Christian population.
Spreading the gospel throughout the world in every
nation,
We are children of Elohim who reigns supreme,
Power to execute whatsoever He wills,
We are the "apple of His eye," and He is El Shaddai,

Whatever we need, He fulfills.
Through Him, we are VIPs, guaranteed a seat
at the Master's table.
If we desire to go higher, He is the bread of life, ready,
willing, and able.
So when dark clouds encompass us and we are unable
to see the sun,
When we grow tired and weary, and the race we can
no longer run,
When the mountains in our lives seem too high to
climb
or large to move,
When it seems as though the rules of this world
set us up to lose,
Know that eyes have not seen, nor ears have heard the
latter
raindrops that will fall.
We have a blessed assurance, our endurance, when our
backs are against the wall.
We have a covenant from Jesus's pain, tears, and blood;
It's certified, sealed, and delivered by our Lord's agape
love,
Blood that is the power over darkness in high places,
The blood that dried tears for two thousand years
from hopeless faces,
Blood that never loses power,

Blood with resurrection strength that can devour and
guarantee,
A blood covenant that gives life more abundantly,
A life that absolutely sets us free.

The Birth of a Poetic Testimony Called "The Greatest Part of Me"

One day, I decided to take a walk in the late evening, just at sunset. The setting sun revealed a beautiful shade of reddish-orange in the sky. The moon shimmered through a large tree at the edge of the beach near the sidewalk. That evening was a gorgeous sight to see. I lived near a beach, and not too far from the lake was a very tall tree.

The moon was shimming directly over it that night. As I walked toward it, I began to feel the presence of God. It was almost as if God tapped me gently on my shoulder and said, "Look up at the tree."

The moonlight reflecting through the branches gave the tree an appearance of power and stability. It towered over the beach; the winds were blowing, soft and warm, through the tree, and you could hear the leaves rustling as they waved back and forth.

While looking up deep into the heart of it, I felt it speak to my spirit. The beauty of it captivated me: the tree was not only tall but also huge in size. The branches were thick. I came to a revelation that this tree was like God.

The roots seemed as though they were planted very deep in the ground, and the tree was very old. I believed if it could talk, it would have many stories to tell. I imagined God being that tree and Jesus being one of the large connecting branches. I was an apple hanging on the branch. I could hear God speaking to my spirit. Holy Spirit allowed me to understand who He was, how He was connected to the Father, and how I was connected to Him. He was inspiring me to write and teaching me His Word at the same time. He inspired me to write a poem called "The Greatest Part of Me." After I wrote it, He revealed to me where it was found in the Bible. And I was shocked to discover how the Bible's message in John, chapter fifteen, related to the poem I had written. I had never read that passage in the Bible because I was new in my relationship with Him.

I am the vine; you are the branches. Whoever lives in me and I in him bears much (abun-

dant) fruit. However, apart from Me [cut off
from vital union with Me] you can do nothing.

John 15:5 (AMPCE),

parentheses and brackets in the original

The Greatest Part of Me

My thoughts are spiritually deep.
One day, I fell into this penetrating sleep.
I dreamt of a tall tree that was strong, wise,
and old; many lives it seemed to hold.
It was the greatest part of me,
Me an apple
Holding steadfast to its branches and taking
no chances.
This tree was love,
It was strong and bold, and many stories it
told.
Though the aging of it was truth and light, it
could not lie.
It stood one hundred stories high.
It was the beginning, forever and
never-ending.
Its power was too overwhelming to imagine.
The tree, the greatest part of me,
And I was proud to be an apple
Holding steadfast to its branches, taking no
chances.

It grew deep into the earth's solid ground.
Thick and strong,
It was righteous and understood wrong.
It taught me how to grow
And what I should know
To become firm and sweet
Because my sweetness was its love.
My firmness was my protection in case I fell.
Its roots spread to the deepest sea to refresh
me.
I was an apple growing on its branches, taking no chances.
I drank from my tree of life.
I hungered for the foods only it supplied
In order that I may stay alive.
I could not eat from any other
Because another
Was neither my father nor my mother.
It is Alpha and Omega.
No other love is greater.
It is the love creator.
The tree, the greatest part of me.
I was an apple holding steadfast to its branches, taking no chances.
Through whistling winds and electrifying
storms,
He keeps me safe and warm.
So I continued to hold on,

I continued growing,
And truly knowing where my branches were
flowing.
My connection was the tree,
The greatest part of me.
Now I was finally ready to be picked out
Away from the others
To sit at the Master's table.
I knew that I was ready
To be used as the food of life.
I was held by human hands.
Consumed by a man in dying need
To be nourished and encouraged
To carry on through life.
I was spiritually free to live in eternity.
I became a tree,
Deep, strong, full of right and understanding
wrong.
It's where I belong:
The tree, the creator of me.

"When you bear (produce) much fruit, My Father is honored and glorified, and you show and prove yourselves to be true followers of mine" (John 15:8, AMPCE; parentheses in the original).

A Song That Reminded Me of My Sister

One day, while listening to a song called "The Wind beneath My Wings," sung by Bette Midler, I wrote a poem that reminded me of my sister. She always looked at me as her hero, and she brought me a fluffy stuffed teddy bear with wings. When you press one of its hands, it will play the song "The Wind beneath My Wings." So I wrote a poem called "Free Love," which is also a testimony about the love of my sister, Sally.

My sister and I grew up fighting, but after we became older, we realized how important a sister's love is and how much we have always loved each other in spite of our past differences.

Sally is now a born-again Christian, filled with the Holy Spirit. For many years, I spoke to my sister about the Lord. One year, she decided to give her heart, but she later went back to the same lifestyle she had before. I did not give up on her, and neither did my mother. We prayed until, one day, she came over for a visit. I knew this visit was going to be different. She stayed overnight. I have morning devotions before I start my day, and I asked her to join me if she desired. I did not pressure her, but God had already gone before me and opened the doors to her heart. I felt led to pray for her, and she said, "I want to be like you."

I knew what she meant and explained to her she needed to repent and rededicate her heart to the Lord. She did with sincerity, and now all she talks about is the Lord. It has only been a few months at that time, and she grew faster than many people who have been saved; eleven years have passed: she is still serving the Lord. I give all the praises to the Lord. Hallelujah!

Free Love

I see colorful crystal blue,
I see love that's loyal and true,
Love that brought us through
Clouds of darkness to fresh morning dew.
We forgave our past and are made anew,
Graced with love long overdue.
Sister love that developed into
Real love that no one could misconstrue,

Free love that is crystal yet royal blue.

Sally, I love you.

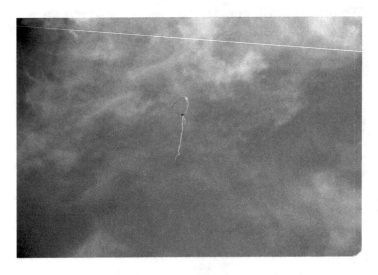

A Hearing Exercise for Writing

Listen to a song in a quiet room. Have a computer or pen and paper ready to write. Do not think about what you are going to say; just allow your spirit to feel from the song. If you sense the words to write, start writing immediately. There is no need to wait until the song finishes. Remember, you are not judging the song; you are not writing about the song. You are only writing whatever you felt while listening to the song. This exercise helps release memories. It will free you from the pressure of trying to think of what to write about. This could lead to a poem or a testimony.

Looking for Love in All the Wrong Places

Jesus answered, "Everyone who drinks this water will be thirsty again, but whoever drinks the water I give him will never thirst. Indeed, the water I give him will become in him a spring of water welling up to eternal life." The woman said to him, "Sir, give me this water so that I won't get thirsty and have to keep coming here to draw water."

John 4:13-15 (NIV)

All humans from all over the world have one thing in common: we all need and want to be loved. It does not matter what racial background or financial status in life we find ourselves in; our basic needs are the same. We have all experienced hurt from a bad breakup or know someone who has.

Most people have experienced getting lost on the road or getting turned around in an unfamiliar building. When we are lost, we stop to first find out where we are, and then we try to find the right direction to our destination, even if it means asking several people to find it. Whenever anyone is involved in a romantic relationship, and it suddenly ends, whether painfully or when both are in agreement, the feeling of depression, hurt, or worthlessness follows. Instead of stopping to restore our emotions, we quickly jump into another relationship. We find it easier to avoid the feeling of hurt by ending up in rebound relationships. Yet later on, as we grow deeper in the new relationship, we discover we moved too quickly and realize we are right back where we started, in another bad relationship.

The bad thing about moving too quickly is the difficulty in walking away once there is intimacy or sexual involvement. According to the Bible, a sexual relationship is like consummating a marriage. When we are involved sexually and romantically with another, we are bound together spiritually, and it becomes more difficult to get free from the spiritual tie.

A Love Search Testimony

I found myself in spiritual ties and found that this was another bad relationship I needed to get out of, but getting out was not as easy as I thought. There I was with this emotional tie and feelings of being a hurt, worthless failure. I had broken up so many times before with this same person, but I found myself coming back because my heart was too involved.

God started to show me spiritually how deep the hole was that I had climbed into. After realizing what I had been doing for years, I called out to the Lord for help and dedicated my heart to Him. He has protected it ever since because I decided to wait on Him. He gave me the strength to break up and the love to enjoy being single.

"Love of God" was written for everyone who is looking for love. Everyone needs to be loved. We cannot replace the love of God with anyone or anything. He is the Love that never fails. Many relationships fail. Love of money can never bring the joy God gives. God's love is called agape love. His death on the cross was intimate at the highest level and cannot be substituted by anyone or anything. The cross is the greatest love letter ever told; He is the lover of our souls. Desperation and loneliness dissipate when we discover the love of God.

Love Search

I went looking for love, so I looked in this alley.
I found it nasty and trifling; I dumped it in the nearest trash,
no, thanks, I'll pass.
I walked around until I came to a better place,
Where there were chandeliers and fine lace.
We drove around in a nice car, never looked at a cheap bar.
Instead, we dined at the Gold Star on caviar.
He looked at me and asked, "Did you get your nails done?"
"That attire is not required for this fine affair, get some better wear."
"Hey! You're using the wrong silverware; please sip your wine."
"No! This is a business trip. I don't have the time."
"Nice, tall heels are what I want to see.

Baby, you must be fine to spend time with me, and
please...pretend that you
have a degree!"
"Well!" I said, "No, you pretend, Mr. X-friend, that you
never met me.
I'll just look for someone compatible."
One looked at me, and instant mental telepathy.
Boy, did we agree! We liked the same food,
We danced the same groove, so we got the same name.
I must admit, after a while, this got rather boring.
Because we played the same sneaky games and drove
each other completely insane.
So I tossed the gold band and went looking for a funny
man.
I just wanted to laugh and have a good time.
Then I met silly Willie.
We would laugh and laugh all the time.
I asked myself, "Would Willie ever get serious?"
One hundred percent laughter kind of made me
curious.
Was he there? Was I there?
Being silly was all Willie knew how to do, so we split
too.
I thought to myself
I'd just be strong and spend my time alone,
But my body wanted to roam, not me!
Just my body, you see.

Later I met Mr. Fine. We had the best time.

He completely swelled my head, and I said;

"Now it can't get any better than this!"

So I would love and give, care and share;

I would always forgive.

I would forgive when I was sad,

I would forgive when he was bad.

I forgave even when I was mad.

I would! I would! Just I,

And only I gave everything I had inside for this bumpy

love ride.

So I cried and cried and cried until I felt like this

sorry-eyed,

Love token, heartbroken, unspoken bag of pain with no

one to blame but shame.

So I found this dark little hole

that was well-hidden, isolated, but not complicated.

I balled myself up in a tight knot like a golf ball,

You know, so I don't fall again, and again

like ditto times two.

Then this light came in, like the tender hands of a

strong

man reaching out for me.

Just like that old movie, Lady Sings the Blues, when

Billy

D. reached out for Diana Ross and asked,

"Do you want my hand to fall off?"

So I looked up with watery eyes with no lies,
and I grabbed that strong hand
And He pulled me up from quicksand.
Because I was sinking fast, totally out of gas,
and this life I was ready to pass,
He spoke to me and said, "Stop majoring in minor
things,
come walk with me, and spread your wings.
For whatever you seek in Me, I will give to you in
poetry."
This light would shine on me like bright lights from a
Christmas tree.
He would hug me, love me, and soothe my head.
He dried up my tears and shined on my lonely bed.
So I welcomed Him home.
Do you know, for the first time, I never felt alone?
He would walk with me, talk with me, dine with me,
and
spend time with me.
This love I will keep forever.
He loves me from the inside out intimately!
Made me want to shout "hallelujah"! Hallelujah!
He taught me intimacy because He looked into me,
see!
This love came from the almighty
Power that dwells above.

When my spirit grows faint within me, it is you who know my way. In the path where I walk men have hidden a snare for me. Look to my right and see; no one is concerned for me. I have no refuge; no one cares for my life. I cry to you, O LORD; I say, "You are my refuge, my portion in the land of the living." Listen to my cry, for I am in desperate need; rescue me from those who pursue me, for they are too strong for me. Set me free from my prison, that I may praise your name.

Psalm 142:3-7 (NIV)

Birth of the Poem "I Desire You"

When I first started to live for Christ, I became spoiled during the first two weeks. I felt the intensity of His presence for the first time in my life. I was overwhelmed with joy. I will never forget when I called my mother, and she said, "Honey, you need to calm down." She thought I was losing it because I was overwhelmed with joy and could not verbalize it.

I had not come to a true understanding, but all I knew was that I felt an awesome sense of peace and love. I had never experienced so much love in my life! I felt as though my eyes were open to see the world for the first time. Everything was absolutely beautiful. I stayed spiritually high for about two weeks. I thought this intense feeling would remain and never leave me.

As time progressed, I continued to live a Christian life, but I became a little lazy in worship and prayer. I stopped praising the Lord. I read the Bible, but it would put me to sleep. I would get up in a hurry because I overslept, or I simply did not take out the time for spiritual meditation or prayer. I would read the Bible as if it was a chore. I started my spiritual journey and desperately needed more understanding. I began to feel sad and was disappointed with God. It felt as if someone ripped out a big chunk of my heart. I could not get the joy back and did not understand why. I prayed a little, but I did not know how to persevere in prayer. I became afraid. I thought He was angry with me and did not want anything to do with me. I put God in a human category.

> For I am afraid that when I come I may not find you as I want you to be, and you may not find me as you want me to be. I fear that there may be quarreling, jealousy, outbursts of anger, factions, slander, gossip, arrogance and disorder.
>
> 2 Corinthians 12:20 (NIV)

We are like babies when we first experience God's presence. He freely gives us grace, but there comes a time when we must not take advantage of God's grace; we must rid ourselves of the baby bottles and start eating meat.

One day during my spiritual development, my church was having a one-week revival. Many pastors from other churches were coming to pray and minister. I could not wait to go; I thought I would get back the feelings I had before with the Lord. I thought I could feel that wonderful love and grace again. But instead, I found myself looking at others cry and praise and become filled with God's glory.

I could not get back that glory I had before because I was angry. I knew something was wrong but did not really understand. I went home feeling jealous and weary, and I began to get angry with God as if He was a boyfriend who stopped calling.

Amazingly, He answered my angry, selfish prayer and said, "You used to worship and praise Me, and now you are far from Me." When I heard His voice in my heart, I cried and could not wait until I had the opportunity to attend the next service. The conviction I felt in my heart was overwhelming. I felt as if God was not pleased with me. I was ready to do whatever it took to get back His grace. I could not wait until I had the opportunity to go again to my church to repent at the altar. At the next service that very same week, I repented.

I cried while asking God to forgive me for being lazy in my daily devotions with Him. One of the members approached me to see if I were okay. While they were talking, I started to feel the spirit of God upon me. I felt the amazing love and grace again. I looked at them and said I was better than okay. I wanted to be left alone. I was once again overwhelmed by His love and grace, and I learned never to take God for granted again.

His presence is indescribable. To be blessed to be in the presence of the almighty God is not by happenstance and should never be taken lightly.

"And ye shall seek me, and find me, when ye shall search for me with all your heart" (Jeremiah 29:13).

I wrote the poem "I Desire You" because I learned how it would be with Him and how it is without Him in my life. You never miss what you never have, but once you have tasted the glory of God, you will come back for more. Through the years, I have grown up spiritually because I love being in the secret place of the Most High. Human love could never compare. God not only loves, but He is also Love, and His love is intoxicating!

I Desire You

I think about You, and all I can do is hope and pray
I remain true.
As I enter into this time of new, I see myself as a part of
You.
I pray every day with all my heart, soul, and mind.
I desire to smell the roses and give You my time
So I may feel the touch of Your gentle breeze,
Tender, intimate moments when I fall to my knees.

We are one like the sun to a flower or a husband to his
wife.
I know with You, I will not only live, but I will have life.
Somehow, You are always in my thoughts,
Continually on my mind.
I envision us being together in harmony somewhere
out of this time.
I need You, Lord, more than I ever needed anything
before.
I want to come closer behind the veil and into the door.
This door, I know I must pay a price,
Your glory is not free.
It is worth the pain and struggle as I enter into the fire,
so please wash me.
You are so real to me; I picture You to be a magnifying
light
That has the form of a man that holds me just right.
Eyes that can see beyond my flesh
and into my soul.
Someone who will always love me and take complete
control.
Crystal red, gold, and a dash of sparkling blue,
Blowing a rainbow of pleasure,
still not equal to the beauty of You.
When I am in Your presence, I feel protected and
loved.
Whenever I am in need, it's always You I'm thinking of.
When I am near You, my desire is to truly live,

I know that comes with my willingness to give.
I surrender my spirit, soul, and mind and die to this
flesh.
I will give You my all, please, Father,
take over and do the rest.
Reach out Your hand, my God, catch me if I fall.
I'll walk on top of the waves and water,
because I desire it all.

Let your hand be ready to help me, for I have
chosen Your precepts. I have longed for Your
salvation, O Lord, and Your law is my delight.
Let me live that I may praise You, and let Your
decrees help me.

Psalm 119:173-175 (AMPCE)

Smelling Exercise for Writing

Find a scented candle or something pleasing to
smell. Inhale its scent, close your eyes, and allow your
natural thoughts to come forth. Do not talk but immediately write down the first thoughts that come to
mind. Your thoughts may travel back in time or may
help you remember something about your current life.
It may inspire you to write a poem, song, or the start of
a story or article.

Try this exercise again until you feel the inspiration that will encourage you to continue to write. It is a very enjoyable experience.

_____

_____

_____

_____

_____

_____

_____

_____

_____

_____

_____

_____

_____

_____

_____

_____

_____

_____

Spiritual Vision

Spiritual vision comes when we are aware of God through His grace. Only then do we see God's hand in everything that was created.

My first experience seeing real beauty was on a misty Saturday morning around 6:00 a.m. I woke up Saturday morning feeling wonderful. I did not have to go to work and started to make myself a cup of coffee. I could not look outside from my apartment because my window faced a large brick building. I felt like getting some fresh air, so I headed outside.

I lived near a beach and decided to take a walk along a large pier across the water. It was misty outside, and a slight chill was in the air. I started to get a wonderful feeling God was with me, and for the first time, I saw mist with spiritual eyes.

I must have overlooked misty days all my life. What I thought of as a dull rainy day, I now saw as a wonderful, glorious day. I walked up to a bench and started talking to God.

A fine mist of small, refreshing droplets gently fell on my face. While sipping my hot coffee, the feel of the refreshing mist was delightful.

I looked up and said to God, "How do You make the clouds spray water like a spray bottle? You are awesome!" He answered me and said, "Write about it."

I started to write what He had given me in my heart. He showed me what I had missed for years. He taught me how to see the beauty of a misty day. So I sat on a bench in the mist and wrote, "Misty Gold."

> God's voice thunders in marvelous ways; he does great things beyond our understanding. He says to the snow, "Fall on the earth," and to the rain shower, "Be a mighty downpour." So that all men he has made may know his work, he stops every man from his labor.
>
> Job 37:5-7 (NIV)

Misty Gold

A chilled misty day
When the rain wants to spray,
When the sun hides away,
When love falls in love,
And real feels the thrill
Of a cool misty morning chill

That's truly, bluely real.
Rain so light, so thin, so fine,
That's sipped like vintage wine
By a delicate flower.
Misty but so mysterious,
Light but, oh, so serious,
Meek but bold,
New but very old,
The flower, a glorious shower,
God's wonderful power, misty gold.

God is the Mastermind of Everything

Our Lord is the Mastermind of everything that exists. He is not a creator; He is The Creator. All talents are from God. Man is made in the image and likeness of God. His image is our spirit, not our flesh. We are creators by nature. This is the reason why many of us can write without taking a course, sing without voice lessons, dance without an instructor, or play various instruments without a music teacher. Think about this for one moment: man created airplanes, but God created birds. The whole idea of flying came from someone watching a bird. Man created a light bulb, but God created the Sun. Man created candy, but God created the sugar cane. Last but not least, God created man.

In the summer of 2000, I went to a women's Christian conference in Atlanta, Georgia. While I was there,

I visited the Atlanta Botanical Garden. My eyes were opened like never before. I began to realize how extremely awesome God's creativity was. I prayed and asked God to give me a poem that would point out His wonderful creativity. I titled it "Mastermind."

> But God made the earth by his power; he founded the world by his wisdom and stretched out the heavens by his understanding. When he thunders, the waters in the heavens roar; he makes clouds rise from the ends of the earth. He sends lightning with the rain and brings out the wind from his storehouses.
>
> Jeremiah 10:12-13 (NIV)

Mastermind

God's great creations,
The Master Designer of the world,
The Maker of gold, diamonds, rubies, and pearls.
The mystery of His creations will surpass the end of time.
Behind all creative thinking, He is the Mastermind.
He created from the ground we walk
To how we talk, from the color of our skin
To the body we were born in.
The Maker of all living animals and plants,

From the elephant to the tiniest ant.
He is the Maker of the tiger,
He gave strength to the bear,
Designed wings for the eagles,
Even the sparrows know He cares.
From the weeping willow to the ginkgo tree,
Creator of the tallest mountain to the deepest blue sea.
All praises to the King who made the morning sun
Never leaving out the dusk at dawn.
This is the Mastermind behind the moonlight's glow,
His creative thoughts designed the falling snow,
The blooming of a rose,
The beauty of a flower
To a strong bucking horse, He gave galloping power.
He created the colorful rainbow after a summer rain.
He placed every star in the sky,
Created every bird for its name.
In the beginning, God!
He created heaven and earth,
Then the creation of spiritual human birth.
The master plan that was created above
Was only through His graceful intimate love.
We were made not for ourselves,
But for Him whom we serve.
He has given us sight to see
Through spiritual vision
Because the purpose of our lives

Is not our own decision.
But to glorify the Maker of the morning sun,
To praise the King who made the dusk at dawn,
To worship the hand that created the moonlight's glow,
The mind that thought of the falling snow,
He who created every sparkling star in the sky,
The One who delivers the Holy Ghost high.
The Maker of purple violets
In a field lovely but free,
The Mother and Father of you and me.
The birth that was thought of before it was born to be.
If we could rejoice in His Word like a bird that sings in
the spring
And mount up like an eagle with mighty wings,
If we could blossom like a flower with growing spiri-
tual power,
If we could shine like the sun on a bright clear day,
And loving, encouraging words in honesty we would
only say,
If we could deliver a sun bliss kiss like the glorious mist
In the heart of one in need of a godly seed,
If we could be like the stars in the sky and focus
Only on our King who dwells up high,
If we could wake up in praise like the morning sun,
And pray to our Lord like the dusk at dawn,
If we could gallop like the horse,
Passing out the power in His Word,

If we could be strong like the eagle
Yet humble like the birds,
If we could draw closer to seek,
We would surely find
The beginning of forever and the Maker of time.
We could mount up like the eagle with mighty wings,
We could sing to our Lord all praises to the King.
We would rejoice the day when infinity meets time,
Magnifying the Glory of our Father, our Creator, the
Mastermind.
In the beginning, God!

"We know that in all things God works for the good of those who love him, who have been called according to his purpose" (Romans 8:28, NIV).

His Plan is Far Greater than Our Plan

God wants us for His purpose and plans. We may not understand His plan for our lives, but we should be ready and willing to be used by Him. There were times the Holy Spirit would lead me to speak at various venues. The Lord would give me a particular poem to read at these events. People would tell me how they were blessed as if the poem was written for them. There have been times when God has given me a message through a poem I would hear later in a sermon. On numerous occasions, I have written poems and found the same message in the Bible. I was unaware until God revealed it to me. God is awesome; He helps me understand the Bible through poetry.

"Do your best to present yourself to God as one approved, a workman who does not need to be ashamed and who correctly handles the word of truth" (2 Timothy 2:15, NIV).

Preparation is always necessary. We must study the Word and spend time with God in prayer and worship. He prepares me when I speak, and He prepares the people to receive His Word. His Word enters their hearts. I am only a token used for His glory. I feel honored to be used by Him. There have been times when I've ministered to lost souls on the street. I remember taking a walk on a pier near my home when I met a young man. He opened up to me as if he had known me for many years. He started talking about his problems in his current relationship. Just when I was about to talk to him about the salvation of the Lord, I felt compelled to recite a poem called "A Hole in Our Soul," which I had written about God delivering me from a bad relationship. We talked for forty minutes, and he said, "I'm going back to church."

"And how can anyone preach unless they are sent? As it is written, 'How beautiful are the feet of those who bring good news'" (Romans 10:15, NIV).

Birth of a Poem Called "A Hole in Our Soul"

There is space in everyone's heart that belongs to God and God alone. When we leave Him out of our lives, we will always feel emptiness or have a strong feeling that something is missing. No matter where you are socially, financially, or physically, there is a need for God, and no matter what we do to fill that void, it will never fill the emptiness because that place belongs to the Lord. We can have all the money in the world, and it will not fill that void. There are many rich and famous people who have the same problems as anyone else who do not have the love of God in their hearts.

In order to love, you must understand this: God is love. He does not do love. He does not need to create love. When He lives in our hearts, we are able to love because He *is* love.

When I was in ungodly relationships, I only had temporary happiness. When the date ended, so did my happiness. I felt empty all over again. I had no joy, no peace, or hope. I was tired of waiting for someone to love me for me. I finally gave up. I cried out to God, angry and desperate. He answered my prayer, and I now have joy that is truly unspeakable, and I have peace that is beyond my understanding. Yes, there are storms from time to time because the rain falls on the just and unjust. I have a shelter I can run to, and His name is Jesus. I was like the woman at the well in John 4:1-30 when God delivered her from the ungodly relationships and filled her heart with His love and joy. She ran to the town and testified to every man she knew about God. Her joy was restored, and out of all the men she encountered, not one was able to give her what Jesus had given her.

The poem "A Hole in Our Soul" will give you a glimpse of what it feels like when your heart needs to be filled with the Lord.

A Hole in Our Soul

There was a hole in our souls.
Tears of pain were rolling down his cheeks.
I was compelled to hold him, but my spirit was getting weak.
So I wiped off his tears and pulled away with fear

Of returning to a past not destined to last.
His desperate crying and pleading
Left my heart bleeding in sorrow,
But I could not and would not go back to yesterday.
I looked forward to a newborn tomorrow.
In desperation, he was trying to make me see
The crying and pleading were only for me.
He did not understand that God had set me free,
Free from tears on my pillow.
If you labeled me a tree,
I would have been a weeping willow.
Free from the pain that remains with a kiss that said
goodbye,
He would always say, "I'll see you soon,"
But I knew it was a lie.
Free from hoping one day he would share his life with
me
Not temporarily but permanently.
Free from never sharing his selfish little world.
I guess it was too hard for him to see me being his only
girl.
He was taking, and I was giving.
Always sex and never really living.
So strange,
But I could see that he really had a love for me,
Deep in a different dimension.
Well! With all the love I was giving,

I guess his heart had to pay attention.
But we still depended on each other to fill this empty
hole
in our souls
That could never be replaced.
So we played part-time house at will,
Pretending and depending that this hole would
somehow
get filled.
All we offered each other was a part-time thrill.
After the last goodbye that was the biggest lie, Ms.
Weeping Willow started to cry.
But this time, she was compelled to pray,
Because she could no longer go on this way.
She asked God if He could take over her life
And please take the pain that was driving her insane.
"Oh, God! If You would just deliver me today,
I'll be or do whatever You say."
She bowed to her knees in such a way
This light from heaven shined directly in that hole
for a permanent stay.
This hole was filled like a cup running over,
And she finally stopped picking at a four-leaf clover.
He showed her love she had never felt before,
Love that would never say goodbye at the door.
Intimate love,
Unconditional love,

Love that can't compete,
Love that would not cheat,
Love that stayed at home,
Love that never left her alone.
Elohim love,
Supreme love,
Love that leaves a soft, pleasant breeze.
Love that kept her travailing on her knees,
The ultimate love that shined through her skin.
That kind of love that loves over and over and over
again!
The love that was in her heart to stay,
Love that kept her from turning back to yesterday.
The love that died on Calvary,
The love that filled that hole and set her heart free.

All night long on my bed I looked for the one my heart loves; I looked for him but did not find him. Scarcely had I passed them when I found the one my heart loves. I held him and would not let him go till I had brought him to my mother's house, to the room of the one who conceived me.

Song of Solomon 3:1, 4 (NIV)

Crucifixion of Jesus

One day during the beginning of my salvation, I watched a documentary about the crucifixion of Jesus Christ. I grew up hearing the story of Jesus being crucified and never really heard it like I heard it on this day.

My eyes and ears were opened to understanding the intense pain and agony Jesus experienced. He was so powerful: all He had to do was speak and not move a finger, and they would have been destroyed. In the Garden of Gethsemane, the soldiers fell down when He answered them, "I am He." I realize if it were not for His divinity, He would have died from all the blows to His head after many soldiers punched and hit Him. I am sure these were not little slaps in the face. Imagine these were strong soldiers. No human, regardless of how strong, could endure what He did without dying.

I realized that He felt what a normal man or woman would have felt as human, but His divinity kept Him from dying until the appointed time. What amazed me the most was all the pain He endured without killing us. He suffered excruciating pain over and over and over again. He felt all the agonizing pain the same as any of us would have felt it. Imagine taking a drug that kept you from dying, and you were continually being crucified and tortured, but you could not die. That is unimaginable for us, but He refused to die until His appointed time; that's unexplainable agape love.

I cried and prayed harder than I had ever before that night, asking the Lord to forgive us. I could not understand why He went through so much to save us. As I meditated on His crucifixion, I saw a vision of a man riding a white horse, charging to save his love from danger. It was like an old love story. I realized it was the greatest love story ever told. It was not the nails that kept Jesus on the cross, but it was the power of His love.

This documentary inspired me to write the poem "Mission Accomplished." This love story makes any love story look like child's play. I wondered: Do we really know what love is? He is love. I thank God for Jesus, who came to show us the power of His love.

> Do not let your hearts be troubled. Trust in God; trust also in me. In my Father's house are many rooms; if it were not so, I would have told you. I am going there to prepare a place for you. And if I go and prepare a place

for you, I will come back and take you to be
with me that you also may be where I am.

John 14:1-3 (NIV)

Mission Accomplished

From heaven, Majesty came
From His mighty throne on high.
He came through everlasting,
Passing every element in the sky,
Passing through the stars and moon,
Through the sun and clouds.
From infinity to time, from life to death.
He came through human life, a mother He created.
He came into a world of sin; He came where He was
hated.
To be placed in swaddling clothes
And to be mocked in disgrace,
He came to be slapped by a band of soldiers
With strong hands to His face.
He was spat on and criticized.
He was hated and mutilated.
He came to be stripped of His robe
As the jealous took His crown.
Spikes embedded in His head
As His blood soaked the sinful ground.

He came for His hands to be hammered to wood He
created;
His feet were nailed down as the pain penetrated.
Spoken words of forgiveness were still bleeding from
His heart.
He came where His veil was ripped and His flesh torn
apart.
Hanging from the nails as His strength slowly
diminished,
He hung His head and died, and the job was only
semi-finished.
He came sinking even lower to the darkest pit of hell,
Taking back the keys to our souls with the power that
prevailed.
He could have called ten thousand angels with mighty
wings of thunder,
Power that could have taken us forever under,
But instead, amazing grace came down, knocking at
our door.
A Knight in shining armor came fighting to save His
love,
Connecting to our spirits, bonding holiness from
above.
He came with mighty love, greater than our wildest
imaginations.
He came healing the sick, raising the dead, miracles,
powerful illustrations.

The Lover of our souls, compassion that's deeper than
the sea,
Royalty came to save us from sin and no greater love
than He.
He came, creating a meeting place where romance will
engulf the air.
It shall be the sweetest taste of honey only faithful
hearts
to share.
The rapture that will lift us up and fuse us back
together,
A master plan to reign with His bride,
When the end of time will meet forever.
He came presenting wine, the blood from His only
Son,
A battle He planned and victory for our souls He won.
The ripping of the veil and the stabbing to His side
Was the opening of the gate for His bride to come
inside.
The keys taken back from the enemy was the trade-off
for our sins,
A gift from our God, the beginning, beginning again.
The rising from the grave was the rising of the sun,
A prepared place of glory, a celebration He had won.
A toast from above, mission accomplished, and a job
well done.

After Jesus said this, he looked toward heaven and prayed: "Father, the time has come. Glorify your Son, that your Son may glorify you. For you granted him authority over all people that he might give eternal life to all those you have given him. Now this is eternal life: that they may know you, the only true God, and Jesus Christ, whom you have sent. I have brought you glory on earth by completing the work you gave me to do. And now, Father, glorify me in your presence with the glory I had with you before the world began."

John 17:1-5 (NIV)

What Has Salvation Saved You From?

Write, in as many words as the space allows, a brief testimony of how being saved has delivered you from destruction.

_____

_____

_____

_____

_____

_____

_____

_____

_____

_____

_____

_____

_____

_____

_____

Our Responsibilty is to Feed the Sheep

When they had finished eating, Jesus said to Simon Peter, "Simon, son of John, do you truly love me more than these?" "Yes, Lord," he said, "you know that I love you." Jesus said, "Feed my lambs."

John 21:15 (NIV)

People are hungry to know the Lord is real today and working in our lives, and it is our responsibility to feed those who are hungry to know. Writing about how we victoriously overcame our pain and sorrow through the help of Jesus Christ will increase our spiritual walk with God and help save other lives.

Becoming a willing vessel is becoming a vessel that God will bless.

As each of you has received a gift, (a particular spiritual talent. A gracious divine endowment), employ it for another as [befits] good trustees of God's many-sided grace [faithful stewards of the extremely diverse powers and gifts granted to Christians by unmerited favor].

1 Peter 4:10 (AMPCE),
parentheses and brackets in the original

Spiritual and Natural Gifts Are from God

We have a responsibility to our Lord and Savior, Jesus Christ, to use our natural talents and spiritual gifts according to His desire and not our own. Everything we are and everything we have belongs to God. There is much reward for obeying God's Word.

Examples of Spiritual Gifts

Apostleship, prophecy, evangelism, pastor-teacher skills, administration, leadership, faith, knowledge, wisdom, exhortation, discernment, ministering, service, giving, tongues, interpretation of tongues, miracles, healing(s) mercy, hospitality. Spiritual gifts are of the Holy Spirit.

Examples of Natural Gifts

Skills of a pianist, guitar player, singer, carpenter, writer, speaker, dancer. Our natural talents are valuable if we use them for the glory of our Lord. They have different functions for building the kingdom of God. For example, a worship leader can obtain various spiritual gifts like discernment and/or encouragement, yet he or she can have the natural ability to sing or play an instrument. A writer can have the spirit of evangelism and prophecy. A dancer can have the spiritual gift of exhortation. They all come together like food and a stove. Food needs the stove to cook it like natural talents need spiritual gifts to glorify God.

"Let the favor of the Lord our God be upon us, and establish the work of our hands upon us; yes, establish the work of our hands" (Psalm 90:17, ESV).

"Whatever you do, work heartily, as for the Lord and not for men, knowing that from the Lord you will receive the inheritance as your reward. You are serving the Lord Christ" (Colossians 3:23-24, ESV).

> Now there are varieties of gifts, but the same Spirit; and there are varieties of service, but the same Lord; and there are varieties of working, but it is the same God who inspires them all in every one. To each is given the

manifestation of the Spirit for the common good.

1 Corinthians 12:5-7 (ESV)

*What Talents or Spiritual Gifts Do You
Have and Use to Glorify God?*

_____

_____

_____

_____

_____

_____

_____

_____

_____

_____

_____

_____

_____

_____

_____

_____

Testimony: A Bar Experience Out of Obedience

I remember many years ago, I spent a lot of time writing an unusual poem called "The Beast That's out of Control." The beast is the tongue.

While writing this poem, all I could think about was a bar that was about a mile away from where I lived. I had never been inside, but I often passed it whenever I was in the area. God continued to speak to my heart about going there that day.

It did not make an ounce of sense to me at the time why He would prompt me to go to a bar. After all, I am a Christian now. Moreover, I never liked bars, even when I lived in sin. I hated the smoky environment. I hated sitting at a bar, waiting for someone to talk to me. Even worse, I felt like a piece of meat on a slab waiting for some guy to choose me out from the rest. Before my salvation, I lived in sin and loved dancing and drinking from time to time, but I just hated bars. I used to like house parties better because I was with people I knew.

I pondered the thought over and over again in my head, *Why would the Lord send me to a bar?* I knew it was the Lord because the poem had everything to do with me going, and it was the Lord speaking to me to write the poem.

The Lord continued to really press upon me to go. I knew it was the Lord without a doubt speaking to me. It was not the first time He gave me a poem with instructions on where I would recite it. Out of fear of not being obedient to God, I reluctantly headed out, walking to that bar and carrying the poem with me.

After entering the bar, I looked around, wondering, *What should I say if someone approaches me?* I did not want to drink and wasn't interested in dancing. Nor was I interested in sitting and listening to the style of music they were playing. All I wanted to know was: how, when, and where I would recite this poem. I stood there dumbfounded; then I saw a sign that read, "Poetry contest, sign up here." I asked an employee what time the contest was, and he said it was going to start within that same hour. I finally could relax a little because I found the how, when, and where to recite the poem. I later started to get nervous because of the message of the poem, "The Beast That's out of Control." *In a bar? The beast is always out of control in a bar, oh my God! People will boo me off the stage,* was my thought.

The contest started after waiting for a half-hour. They called many people before me. All people who were called to the microphone were using so much vulgar language I forgot it was poetry. You name it; they said it: swearing, profanity, cursing in poetry. I never knew poetry could be so difficult to listen to. I was not in a position to judge because before salvation, I, too, cursed from time to time whenever I was angry. So I bit down and got through it. I was afraid to recite the poem, but I was more afraid not to obey God. I was finally called to the microphone.

And the MC said to the audience, "If you like the poems, pop your fingers. If you know the next rhyming word, you could say it out loud before the speaker does. If you don't like the poem, stomp your feet." This was not a good place to recite a poem because you could be exposed to embarrassment and public humiliation just from the sound of stomping feet. What really amazed me was the people using vulgar profanity did not receive any negative stomping of feet from the audience. I said to myself, "I know they will stomp me off the stage; plus, I am a Christian, and my poem might even sound corny to them. Oh God, help me!" I cried silently.

I heard my name: "Now we will welcome Ms. Lena Edwards to the mic." Needless to say, I was very nervous. While I recited the poem "The Beast Who Was out of Control," silence filled the air. It was so quiet that if a small pin the size of a needle dropped on the floor, you could hear it. There were no sounds of popping fingers, no stomping of feet, nothing at all, just silence. Once I completed reciting the poem, I had a strong desire to leave right away, but the Lord prompted me to stay awhile. When the judges called the winner, believe it or not, it was me. The prize was twenty dollars, and they were going to present it to me before the bar closed.

I walked out. I could not bear to stay another minute in the smoky environment, plus I felt very awkward. Everyone was staring at me as if I was the judge who convicted them. Well, when I think about it, I was the voice of God, and He is the judge. I was very happy when it was over, but even happier that I obeyed God. The money at that time did not matter because I won something much more important: a lesson in obedience.

The Beast Who Was out of Control

There's this beast that has no name,
He spits out words that search for pain,
Words that cut razor-sharp,
Words that shoot fiery arrows and dart,
Aggravating, discriminating, irritating, and bold,
Rootless, outspoken, and out of control.
It's that beast that has no name,
He uses the tongue to play deadly games.

Be careful if you have a gift to boldly speak out:
Anger crouches at the door to make that boldness
curse and shout.
The tongue can become a powerful gun.
It loves drive-by shooting, just making fun.
Remember, children absorb, and they have tongues,
too.
They learn what to say by listening to you.
The beast has a game he calls "tit for tat,"
Ruthless words of, "I got you back, attack for attack."
Cursing out of control, crying temper tantrums
Are the beast's favorite song he calls his national
anthem.
He uses your tongue to upset the opposition
As he lays back and enjoys the fighting competition.
Mindless drivel, uncaring, unashamed, and bold
Is victory for the beast because you're out of control.
The beast kills, steals, and destroys by using words that
drive you insane.
The secret to conquering the beast and beat him at his
own game
Is to take every angry thought into captivity and call on
Jesus's name,
Stop to repent and forgive, then speak words you de-
sire to be.
The power of God's Word will tame your tongue and
set you free.
Your spirit will illuminate like the glistening sun.

The beast that was out of control will take off and run.
You will think first, then speak thoughtfully and slow.
Your tongue will speak to encourage, and your spirit
will glow.
Your tongue will speak, and you will suddenly say
Words like "God bless you" and "Have a pleasant day."
Forgive me for speaking, ruthless and bold,
That unknown beast tried to take complete control
He wanted to destroy me and take my soul.

Testimony: The Car Accident

While traveling back home from visiting my mother, I missed my exit to the highway that led to my home, so it took me twice as long to get home. I had a trunk full of groceries because I did a little shopping before leaving her town. I was a bit tired. When I finally came to the exit near my home, there was a car in front of me exiting as well. This particular exit was one that required me to check my side view mirror to see if there was any oncoming traffic. As I proceeded ahead after checking the mirror, I noticed the car driving in front of me suddenly stopped. I hit my brakes too late and bumped the car, slightly denting his bumper.

I gestured for the driver to move ahead so that we could get out of the way of the oncoming traffic. I was upset with myself for not being more careful. I was hoping the driver of the car I bumped was okay. He moved ahead, made a right turn, and I pulled up in front of him.

He got out of his car, and I asked him if he was okay. He did not say anything at all. I asked again repeatedly, "Are you okay?" I apologized, and still, he said nothing at all. He walked around his car to check for damages, then he got back into his car and called the police station nearby. The police called for a state trooper because the incident was off the expressway. All highway accidents require state troopers. He told me they would be a while and got back into his car, and I got back in mine.

One hour later, a tough-looking female state trooper got out of her car. She walked up to the driver of the other car, and they talked while I waited. After speaking to the other driver, she approached me and started yelling. She said, "If this man is injured, you may be in big trouble, lady!" I felt like this day had hit an all-time low point for me. I thought, Why is this trooper so angry? Is this the first time she has investigated an accident? I tried to explain, but she did not want to hear anything I had to say. She asked for my license and insurance card. After writing out a police report, she left. Immediately, another man showed up for the other driver, and they sat in his car, talking. The driver I hit got out of his car and told me I made him miss his driving class; he was injured and had to see his doctor. I wanted the other driver to know that I did not bump him intentionally, and again, I apologized.

I sat in the car shocked, tired, and desperately wanting to get home after the two-hour drive. I was not sure if the driver was really injured from the bump. I could only hope and pray he was okay. I knew I was wrong, but I was also aware that some people lie about injuries. I only prayed that he was not one of them. Nevertheless, this case looked hopeless. I was devastated, and I prayed in my car.

"Oh God, You know my heart. I did not intentionally bump the other car. Oh God, I hope he is okay, and I pray he does not lie. Please, Lord, I know I do not deserve it, but please grant me grace for this situation, please don't allow this man to sue me."

Needless to say, I had a court date. I had to go to work during the week of my court date. I had time to go to work first before my court appearance. I reminded my boss that I was in a car accident and needed to go to court that day. He asked what happened, and I told him. He immediately said, "You will definitely lose this case, so get ready for it." I knew it was not possible to win according to the law, but I believed in a higher authority. I replied, "God will be with me, and I am going to win." I spoke out of faith. Thankfully, the court was not far, and my boss allowed me to go on my lunch break.

When I made it to court, I hoped that the driver of the other car would not come, but lo and behold, he showed up, came in, and had a seat in front. I whispered to God, "I still believe You." Later after standard court proceedings, he was the first one the judge called. When he walked up to the judge, the judge proceeded to ask him questions. After a few minutes, I heard the judge repeatedly ask, "Are you sure?" The driver said, "I am." The judge called my name, and I walked up and stood next to the other driver. The judge looked at me and said, "You are very lucky; this young man decided to drop all charges." I was relieved, surprised and happy.

The driver of the other car began to walk quickly out of the courtroom, and I ran after him to thank him. I said to him, "Thank you very much for dropping this case." He looked back at me while still walking and quietly said, "God told me to do it." As I walked back to my car, I prayed, "Lord, I thank You so much. What would I do without You?"

I quietly replied to the judge's statement and said, "That was not luck; that was my Lord interceding for me." I made it back to my job within the hour; I did not lose any pay. I walked into my boss's office and said, "I won!" He looked at me, surprised, and said, "That is amazing!" I said, "That was God. I told you He would be with me."

"What, then, shall we say in response to these things? If God is for us, who can be against us?" (Romans 8:31, NIV).

Women Are Special to God

There are many special women in my life who I look up to. The first one is my mother. I miss her. She had a way of making each one of my sisters and brothers feel as if we were her only child. We were all treated like we were special. She was married to an abusive man, and growing up in Mississippi was not easy during her time. Yet, she emerged through the help of God to be a wonderful wife, mother, and child of God. I will never forget how she would walk for ten to fifteen blocks to care for her elderly friends. She would wash their clothes, cook, and still make it home on time to cook for her own family. She was also very helpful at the church we attended. I do not understand how she did it all.

I also have a wonderful daughter who is a working wife and has a child. She takes very good care of her family. She owns a family business with her husband,

and they both also work their regular job. She, too, is a master taskmaster.

There are wonderful women at my church, family and friends, to whom I dedicate this poem. This is my testimony of how precious women are to the kingdom of God. I have been inspired to write by so many inspiring women. Thank you, God, for making me a woman.

"So God created man in his own image, in the image of God created he him; male and female created he them" (Genesis 1:27).

Enmity

Man and Woman
God designed women and men to praise and worship
Him
and Him alone.
He made them for His own.
Adam's eyes were amazed as he gazed at such
a marvelous design:
Eve captivated and blew Adam's mind.
God made her to be a mother and wife and live a
fulfilling,
wonderful life.
He took His time when He designed woman's
unique qualities,
Giving her the ability to be a multi-taskmaster;
He wanted her to handle many responsibilities.

He made her to reproduce, bear fruit,
He created her to be of good use,
She was a piece of art with many complex body parts.
He made her sensitive and gave her a big heart.
He crafted and molded woman like an expensive
piece of art.
He designed her to be the mother of nations
She never knew what she would go through to crush
the devil's head
When God said,
"I will put enmity between you and the woman, be-
tween your seed and her seed;
He shall bruise your head, and you shall bruise his
heel."
This reality became real,
The process for a transformation to birth kings for
nations.
How anxiously she waited with much anticipation for
a great celebration,
but first to come were
Pain and frustration led by irritation that called for
much
needed spiritual medication.
Birth pains came through her beautiful frame.
Getting up on sleepless nights to quiet tears from
hungry
baby cries,
From bloodshot eyes,

Some with husbands who were never quite right,
Disciplining children, trying to spare the rod was a
twenty-four-hour job.
Loving, giving, and holding on to living.
There are times when she cannot breathe, when she
falls to
her knees to pray
Because one bad day would nearly take her
breath away
But God made her this way to take a lick but
continue to tick.
When the pressure and hot flashes were
Melting her false but true lashes,
Being deceived by long weave, trying to please
Her man with a remote control in his hands,
Forever on diets yet continued to expand
From so many worldly demands,
Her life was a roller coaster without brakes,
And she would take and take
But wise enough to take time out anyway,
She knew she needed time to pray.
She would wail and cry
She opened her heart with all of her issues
Filling the floor with wet tissues.
Her Maker was touched by her infirmities.
In the presence of her King,
In a brief silent moment, she heard a soft voice say,
"The water is before you; drink, it is free."

He said that the living water already lies inside,
Springing up like a root from dry ground.
When she feels weak, filled with hopelessness and
despair,
God said, "Thy Maker is thy husband, I love you, and I
care."
Then she knew if only she could touch the hem of His
garment,
She would be made whole under control, humble yet
bold.
Her Lord told her to reach out and grab it; her joy was
already there.
With her strength, she pushed through the madness,
overcame her sadness,
She released her tears from broken years;
He renewed her mind and gave her peace.
He took her despair to make her love again and care.
She stumbled across His Word that read, "The joy of
the Lord is my strength."
It says sorrow may last for a night, but joy comes
in the morning.
Then she realized the morning is not just a time of day;
It was not a long wait for Him to wipe her tears away.
Morning comes when her prayer turns into thanks
And thanks turn to worship and worship to praise.
Then she became amazed by His glory,
And like the woman at the well, she was a witness
for His stories.

Like Naomi, she returned to the place of her birth
to restore her glory.
Like Ruth, she found the truth, made a decision to
follow,
Where He was, she went.
Risking her own life like Esther, she interceded for her
people with courageous strength.
Like Sarah, she became and proclaimed to be the
mother
of many nations.
She recognized she was God's creation.
She began to serve like Martha and worship at His feet
like Mary.
Contrary to what others may think, she believed
and received.
She believed in Him and what He has done to set her
free.
Because He died, she lived, because He gave, she now
gives.
He is her husband and lover.
He is her strength and cover.
He is her doctor and provider.
In the darkness and storms, He is her righteousness
and guide.
She shall mount up like an eagle from her mountain
with wings.
She shall sing sacrifices of praise to fulfill her cloudy
days.

He gives peace that's beyond her understanding
But close enough to reach.
She has joy even when things are not going her way.
She praises Him anyway, whether the skies are sunny
or gray.
She learns to commit and never quit.
She loves Him, and He truly loves her.
It's He that set her free
When she had no ability to see.
When she became dry and thirsty,
She drank that which is freely given
From the fountain of life and joyful living.
She praised Him until worship leaked from her pores
and
through her soul,
She praised Him until He took complete control.
Then she raised her stilettos with her freshly painted
but pretty toes,
Bringing her feet high, came down with a lightning
sound, crushed the devil's head
And said, "Enmity is dead!"
Because He is strong, I can!
Because He is, I am Woman!

Walking by Faith
Testimony

Faith comes when we develop a relationship with God.

We must try to know Him for who He is. Many times, we seek God for what He can do for us rather than seeking Him to know who He is. Seek the Giver, not the gift. He is everything we need in life. The Bible says in Matthew 6:33, "But seek ye first the kingdom of God, and his righteousness; and all these things shall be added unto you."

Our faith increases as God walks us through our storms to develop our character. He knows what will grow us, and He will never leave us. The Bible says in Hebrews 13:5, "Let your conversation be without covetousness; and be content with such things as ye have: for he hath said, I will never leave thee, nor forsake thee."

I will never forget when the IRS audited me. I trusted an accountant to file my taxes. I hired him every year for four years. I was unaware he was cheating on my taxes. He felt if I received a big return, he could ask for a larger amount for filing my taxes. I partially blame myself for not paying enough attention to the details. Five years later, I was audited by the IRS demanding a very large lump sum of money that I did not have. The amount was over $13,000. I was totally upset. If that was not bad enough, I received a letter from my mortgage company that stated I was behind in my escrow account by $800, and I needed to pay that right away in order for them to pay my home tax bill. Both letters came on the same day. I looked at the letters, dropped them down on my dining room table, and walked up the stairs to my prayer room. I cried out to God, asking for help.

I came back downstairs after prayer and felt a tug in my spirit to call my mortgage company. A very rude young lady who answered the phone assured me I was in debt by $800 and needed to pay it right away. I did not want to get upset, so I asked to speak to her manager. The manager got on the phone. I had the letter of debt in my hand and read it to her. She got off the phone for a few minutes, and when she came back, she said, "Ms. Edwards, you do not owe us $800; we owe you $800. Your escrow is short by $500, but we did not know what to do with the extra money. So we wanted to know if you would like us to apply $500 to the escrow." I said that was wonderful. She apologized for the letter and stated, "I will mail you a check for the balance of $300."

I felt my faith increasing at that very moment. I had enough courage to call the IRS office.

They asked me for a ton of paperwork, mostly documents I did not have. I gathered as many documents as I could find and mailed those to them. Time passed, and I had not heard from them in over a month. A week or two later, I received a postcard from the post office asking that I pick up a certified letter. I picked up the letter, and it was from the IRS office, stating: "We have resolved your case, and you now owe us $3,000." I was happy and started thanking God in the car for bringing down the payment to a lesser amount. I did not have $3,000. I was happy, but at the same time, I was a little confused.

I spoke to the Lord again, "Lord, I am grateful, but you are God; You could get rid of all of it." As I continued to drive, I heard the voice of God saying, "Can You trust me for the rest?" I said, "Yes, I can," and He said, "Call them again." I said to myself, "Call again?"

It sounded so crazy after they had already stated in the letter they have resolved my debt, and now I owed a lesser amount. I made a choice to trust God in spite of the situation. He had already shown Himself strong in my life many times, and I was not going to stop believing now. I got to work, and the first thing I did was calling the IRS office after asking my boss. My case manager picked up the phone. I did not know exactly what I was going to say, but I simply said to her that I did not believe I owed them the $3,000. She asked me to hold for a few minutes while she checked my file. I was nervous, hoping she did not return to the phone with an attitude. But a few minutes later, she picked up the phone and said, "Ms. Edwards, you owe us nothing; your balance is zero, and your file is closed." I was shocked, surprised, and overjoyed. I wanted to quickly get off the phone, so I said, "Thank you," and hung up the phone.

I praised my God to the highest on that day. I will never forget tossing both letters on the table. I felt hopeless until I prayed and asked the Lord to help me. I was upset, but I did not give up on God. I had plenty of hope.

I believe there is nothing God cannot do. The Bible says,

> Then the disciples came to Jesus privately and said, "Why could we not cast it out?" He said to them, "Because of your little faith. For truly I tell you, if you have faith the size of a mustard seed, you will say to this mountain, 'Move from here to there,' and it will move; and nothing will be impossible for you."
>
> Matthew 17:19-20 (NRSV)

My mountain moved. I am living proof it works!

Faith Is

Faith is not religious echoes of repeated I believes:
I believe, I believe, I believe...
It does not worry or stress.
It is not tension or grief.
Faith has the power to move mighty clouds of thunder
Faith walks with assurance. Faith does not wonder.
Faith is not a "think positive" book or an up-righteous look.
Faith is a seed in time of need planted by our Lord.
It is that connection with God in one accord.
Faith is a desire that grows with storms and fire.
Faith has a will that wants to climb higher and higher.
It burns with desire because it hungers to achieve
When you know that you know.
When your heart cries out, "Believe!"
Faith feels freedom in free.

Faith leaps over boundaries of impossibility.
Faith is trusting truth, knowing it will surely
come to pass.
Faith has vision that can see a vision that will
last.
Faith is not procrastination or hesitation; it
moves even in fear.
It grows with diligence and the seeking to be
near.
Faith does not murmur, complain, cry, strain,
or beg.
It is joy and peace of knowing what is ahead.
Shadrach, Meshach, and Abednego—
Faith is what set them free.
The hottest fiery flame became a cool breezy
sea.
It shines a light in the darkness and calls the
devil a liar.
That kind of faith takes the hot out of the fire.
Daniel's faith and prayers brought forth God's
mighty power.
Unbelievers knew it was Daniel's final hour.
But his faith closed the mouths of hungry sav-
age beasts,
Stood like a rock, and brought angry lions to
peace.

Abraham's faith was overflowing his trusting cup;
He gave his only son, knowing that God could raise him up.
Believing in God is always addition and never deduction.
He is the author and finisher of faith
And the answer to every unanswered question.
He can bring forth wisdom from the lame and dumb.
He is God of what is, what was, and what will come,
The Creator of our destiny, before we were born to be,
Allowing storms to build the faith that creates reality.
Faith will make a vision come to pass at God's appointed time.
Faith must stand the test of hopelessness and unbelieving minds.
It is impossible to please God without faith, hope, or trust.
Faith is not a maybe; faith is a must.
Only one fish and five loaves—there were thousands that were fed.
Faith put life back in the body of Lazarus being four days dead.

Faith is the key to the door to eternal life.
Faith cut into the darkness like a jagged-edge
knife.
Faith walks on top of the water,
Faith split the Red Sea,
Made the lame walk,
Healed diseases, and set the captives free.
Faith brought new birth into Sara, who was
far beyond her childbearing years,
Brought the wall of Jericho tumbling down.
Faith brings forth happy tears.
Noah built an ark for the mighty thunder of
rain.
All was lost, but the faithful at heart remained.
A woman healed from an issue of blood
By just the touch of Jesus's robe.
A man who lost his entire family and every-
thing he owned,
His body was stricken with boils and pain; he
carried
A heavy load, but he earned a double return
More than all the riches and gold,
A mighty believer of God, this man of faith
was Job.
Now faith is the substance of things hoped for
And the evidence of things not seen.
Faith does not walk unsure;

Faith flies in on eagle's wings.

Standing on His promises and making a final decision,

Studying, worshipping, and praying will give you a spiritual vision.

Seek, and you will find, knock, and the doors will open.

Faith is an action word that moves as it is spoken.

Faith is the test that makes a testimony.

Faith is a living experience; faith can never be phony.

Faith will shine belief in an unbelieving mind.

Faith falls asleep in a storm and takes the ticking out of time.

Faith is like a telephone call to God that He will surely hear.

Faith is what you need when seeking to be near.

Faith is not a wish, a doubtful maybe, a question, or a quiz.

Faith pleases God because faith believes God is!

"He replied, 'If you have faith as small as a mustard seed, you can say to this mulberry tree, "Be uprooted and planted in the sea," and it will obey you'" (Luke 17:6, NIV).

Debt Came Knocking at My Door Again

My daughter and son-in-law are executive chefs.

They can really cook, and I know: I am a living guinea pig. They use me for a sample taster, and I feel like I have the best job in the world. I had the privilege of tasting all kinds of international foods that were pleasing to my taste buds.

One day I decided to try out one of the recipes they cooked for me in the past. The recipe required me to add shrimp. I love shrimp, so I added more than the recipe required. I made more than I should have made. I ended up eating a lot of leftovers, a recipe loaded with shrimp. I did not realize I was eating entirely too many shrimp, and my cholesterol increased. At one point while working, I thought I was going to have a heart attack.

I drove myself to the hospital. The doctor repeatedly stated I was most likely a candidate for a heart attack because of my age, gender, and race. I explained to him that I was not having a heart attack because I was speaking in faith. I said that I had too many shrimp. I also called the devil a liar. After keeping me overnight and doing a series of tests, the end result was that I was healthy as a bull, and I had a lot of gas and had to take an over-the-counter medication.

I received a $2,500.00 bill later, which was the balance my insurance did not cover. After receiving the bill from the hospital, I received another IRS bill; this time, it was for $8,000.00. I had more faith than I had in the past, but this test was harder than before because I had to believe more.

The first bill I attacked was the IRS office. As before, they asked me for various documents—sixty-five pages, to be exact. I jumped through many hoops to get all the documents. I finally retrieved most of them and sent them off to the IRS office. Later during the month, I received a letter stating they had not received any of my documents. I called and explained I faxed them, and I mailed them as well. They insisted they did not have them. I checked the address and fax number and sent them again. Two months passed. I called them, and they still indicated they did not have my documents. I was furious.

I could not believe the IRS office could be so incompetent. I insisted on speaking to a manager.

The manager seemed to be friendly and asked if I could fax it once more directly to him.

Once again, I faxed sixty-five pages and mailed them as well. This task was difficult because it cost money to continue to print copies and fax. Moreover, I had to ask my boss to fax them from work. He allowed me to do it. I waited for two months and still had not heard anything from the IRS office.

I later called the hospital to make arrangements for the $2,500.00 hospital bill that I could not afford to pay. The hospital gave me an appointment to come in. I remember going to work that same day. The Lord spoke to me and said, "Call your insurance company." I spoke with them prior to coming to work, and they sent me all the bills they had to pay from the hospital. They told me they were not responsible for the rest. The $2,500.00 sum was my responsibility. But if God tells me to do anything, I try not to question but just do it. I called the insurance company, spoke to a receptionist, and she transferred me to a billing clerk. When the billing clerk asked for my name and insurance number, she explained to me she was glad I had called because she was going to send me a letter stating not to pay any bills to the hospital because the hospital did not get authorization to perform so many tests as they did on me. They stated they were not liable to pay them, and neither was I. I asked her if she could give me that in writing. Later I received a letter stating everything she explained on the phone. I sent the letter to the hospital, and my debt was over.

Now getting back to the IRS: I had not heard from them in a while, and I was afraid to call because I did not want to hear, "We do not have your documents." So I never attempted to call them. One day, God asked me, "What are you afraid of?" I replied, "Lord, I am tired." He said, "Call them." Out of faith, I called. I spoke with a man, and he pulled my file, and lo and behold, he stated that my file was closed and I did not owe the IRS the bill of $8,000.00. Hallelujah! God paid another debt, $10,500.00 total. How awesome is that! He is awesome if you have faith, trust, and obey His voice.

In conclusion, be strong in the Lord [be empowered through your union with Him]; draw your strength from Him [that strength which His boundless mightless might provides]. Put on God's whole armor [the armor of a heavy-armed soldier which God supplies], that you may be able successfully to stand up against [all] the strategies and the deceits of the devil. For we are not wrestling with flesh and blood [contending only with physical opponents],

but against the despotisms, against the powers, against [the master spirits who are] the
world rulers of this present darkness, against
the spirit forces of wickedness in the heavenly
(supernatural) sphere.

Ephesian 6:10-12 (AMPCE),
parentheses and brackets in the original

Has God ever pulled you out of a dreadful situation?
Write it down:

_____
_____
_____
_____
_____
_____
_____
_____
_____
_____
_____
_____
_____

A Two-Way Conversation

I've been to a place where the flames were hot.
I questioned if I would make it or not.
I've been to a tense place of stress, pressed for time
and restlessness.
I was at a place to take a final exam for a serious test.
I was unable to know how much I could take,
I even stumbled and made some careless mistakes.
I felt fragile and thought for a moment I could break.
I cried at times, and times I could not take it another
day.
Struggling through flames, I called out His name, but
He had
nothing to say.
He squeezed and teased and shaped me in such a way
He felt like the potter and I the clay.
I would get angry at times and did not want to pray.
It was those times He seemed millions of miles away.
I developed a thirst for Him like a deer panting at a
brook.
I was becoming dry and hungry from all the beating I
took.
I hated to wait; my patience was tried, so I swallowed
my pride and held on for the ride.
I felt as if I was buried and dead, but I was protected by
the
blood to resurrect inside.

I've been to the potter's house where I was mashed,
crushed, and squeezed.
This place of reconstructing and molding brought me
pleading on my knees.
"Oh, Lord!" I cried, "Wash away the past that wants to
keep me behind,
Wash away the stress, worry and smooth out the age
lines."
"Come a little closer, my beloved, so you will hear:
I have sweet words I would like to whisper in your ear,
Come freely drink of water that will refresh your soul,
Drink of the fountain that will make you whole.
I speak softly; you must come closer to hear
My sound is profound; with Me, there is no stress or
fear.
The last will be the first, and the first will be the last.
It's a new day, and the old troubles have passed.
I am the Lord of Hosts; I have power over every
situation.
Come closer, my child, and hear this revelation:
The earth is my footstool, and you are the apple of my
eye.
I have broken every dark soul tie.
You shall mount up like my eagles; I have given you
keys
to open every door.
You see, my beloved, you have not been down
this path before.

You have the power to tread over every serpent
and grace to win.
The veil is ripped, you're ready and equipped,
but you must enter in.
The curtains are open; the show is about to start.
The world is my stage, and you all have a special part.
My blood was not only to wash you and set you free,
My blood was molding you for a day of jubilee.
This time is a time of blessing, so stand up and cheer—
They will know that I am God, that time is near.
I know that the world is going down a slow hill.
You are in the world, but your home is above.
I have lavished you with blessings and love.
Wait and stand like my eagles and have no fear,
Get ready to receive—the latter rain is here."

The Final Hour

The clock is ticking; we're running out of time.
The walls of Jericho are strongholds of the mind.
But God has formed His people for this time and
season:
"We are not here by chance; we are here for a special
reason.
The clock is ticking; the enemy knows it's eleven
fifty-nine.
He is sending his legions to try to conquer our minds,
Pacing two and fro, seeking whom he can devour."
God has given His people invincible power.

We, the people of God, must put on our helmet of
salvation.
As the salt of this earth, we are here to save this nation.
Put on the breastplate of righteousness and running
shoes.
To win this race, preach the gospel and spread the good
news,
Having a shield of faith to block the arrows and darts.
The enemy is after our minds,
Fighting to stop the beat in our hearts.
Hold on, be strong, don't give up or quit:
Tomorrow, we will hold up a torch
That God has already lit.
Hold up your lights in the darkness
Without trembling and without fear.
God will never leave or forsake us,
He is always near.
"Touch not my anointed and do my prophets no harm;
The battle is not yours, so don't be alarmed."
Warning for those who get in God's way,
Warning to those that do not obey,
Warning to those He has called but have gone astray.
It is better to never have known Him than to slip away.
Heaven and earth shall pass away, but God's Word will
stand.
Put your faith in His Word and your life in His hands.
His divine purpose and plan shall surely come to pass.

The storms are but for a short while, and they will not
last.
For His chosen, there is a purpose.
For every purpose, there is a plan.
For every plan, there is a season.
For every fire, there is a reason.
Wait on the Lord, don't worry
Or dash your foot against a stone.
His ways are not like ours, so have faith and be strong.
The clock is ticking its final hour.
The show is about to start.
The enemy is about to be destroyed.
Open your mind; give God your time.
Jesus is coming for His bride with a clean heart.

In His Presence is Everything We Need

He who dwells in the shelter of the Most High will rest in the shadow of the Almighty. I will say of the LORD, "He is my refuge and my fortress, my God, in whom I trust." Surely he will save you from the fowler's snare and from the deadly pestilence. He will cover you with his feathers, and under His wings you will find refuge; his faithfulness will be your shield and rampart. You will not fear the terror of night, nor the arrow that flies by day.

Psalm 91:1-5 (NIV)

I have a prayer room in my home I dedicated to God when I first purchased my home. It's a special place to give Him my undivided attention, a place to cry, to thank and praise Him.

At times, it is hard to leave because of the heaviness of His presence. It is a place where I learn to appreciate Him for who He is and not just for what He does. I love Him, and it's a place where I embrace Him; He is my spiritual lover.

I hope and pray that everyone who has claimed the Lord as his or her Savior will search for those intimate moments when you come to an intimacy where it is no longer hard to pray, a time when you don't need music, a time when there is less of you and more of Him. Even as I write these words, I find myself missing Him.

At times in our lives, we get so busy and so caught up in our daily activities we forget to give Him our undivided attention. I have come to a place in my life where I must have those moments. God wants to show Himself as being real in our lives. But He must be sought after. His Word declares,

> Ask, and it shall be given you; seek, and ye shall find; knock, and it shall be opened unto you: For every one that asketh receiveth; and he that seeketh findeth; and to him that knocketh it shall be opened. Or what man is there of you, whom if his son ask bread, will he give him a stone? Or if he ask a fish, will

he give him a serpent? If ye then, being evil, know how to give good gifts unto your children, how much more shall your Father which is in heaven give good things to them that ask him?

Matthew 7:7-11

How can we talk about someone we do not know? Isn't that why we are here to be His disciples, to teach others about Him? To tell them how He has affected us in our own individual lives? To tell others about what He has done in our lives so that those who don't know Him get the desire to know Him? He wants us to be fishers of men. This is what He told Peter in Matthew 4:19: "And he saith unto them, Follow me, and I will make you fishers of men."

I find that when people fall in love, we talk about that person day and night. We even make others sick of listening to us talk about the same person day and night. When we share God, we share someone who can be shared with the entire world. God is big enough to love all of us and make each one of us feel the intimate one-on-one encounter with Him. Imagine being in love with God. "Thou wilt keep him in perfect peace, whose mind is stayed on thee: because he trusteth in thee" (Isaiah 26:3).

In His Presence

In His presence is fullness of joy and glory,
In His presence is my life story.
In His presence, He touches the depths of my heart,
That part that no one else could feel because His love is
so real.
In His presence, I am His love, and He is everything to
me.
Nothing else matters, you see, because I am indeed
free.
In His presence, His light shines on my heart,
A soft, warm breeze that keeps me glowing in the dark.
In His presence is the rock on which I stand.
He is the lover of my soul, and my life is in His hands.
In His presence, there is no pain, just the pouring of
rain
That washes my brain with the peace of mind
Only the eagles can define.
In His presence is fullness of joy,
I am just a kid with a brand new toy.
In His presence is a new day.
In His presence, my tears are washed away.
In His presence, I can walk another mile.
In His presence, I can smile and rest for a while.
In His presence, my eyes flood with tears.

In His presence, He restores all my broken, stolen years
of pain.
Only a flower remains:
I can sing,
I have wings,
I can dance,
Have real romance.
In His presence, I can be me.
In His presence, I can see.
In His presence, no one else is around:
Just the sound of an angel that sings
As I am caught up under His wings.
No weapon formed can prosper.
I can stand on my rock.
There is no ticking of clocks.
I can fly; I can even die in His arms
When I am in His presence.

A Childhood Testimony (the Sound of Barking)

God chose us before the earth was created. He already knew what we would go through in life. Even when we are children, He rescues us from the enemy, even before we are fully aware of Him. He makes ways for us to escape sin. His eyes are always on His chosen. We are a chosen generation, and it is commanded of us to produce fruit. It's all about seedtime and harvest. We are the seed of Jesus Christ, He is the seed that was crucified and buried, and we are His fruit. Through time and development, we, too, produce fruit. We are commanded to be disciples and tell others about Jesus in our lives.

It is simply amazing to know that God has always watched over us, starting from our mother's womb. He chose us; we did not choose Him. Our "free will" is actually God's divine sovereignty.

> Ye have not chosen me, but I have chosen you,
> and ordained you, that ye should go and bring
> forth fruit, and that your fruit should remain:
> that whatsoever ye shall ask of the Father in
> my name, he may give it you.
>
> John 15:16

I was attending grammar school. I think I was in sixth grade at the time. I was walking home alone from school. I do not remember many children being with me. I may have come home early because I was not feeling well, or maybe I just walked faster than the other kids. Whatever it was, I remember passing by a large vacant lot. I turned my head, looking towards the empty lot, and there seemed at least ten to fifteen dogs standing around at the end of the lot on the opposite side.

One of the dogs saw me walking and started barking. Before I could quickly walk past, he started running after me. I looked around and saw all of the dogs were chasing me and barking at the same time. I was terrified and ran into an open gate of someone's home. Unfortunately, the gate was broken, and it swung open. The latch on the gate was broken, and to make matters worse, the front door of the home was locked. I had nowhere to run.

The house did not have any open doors that I could run into. I was so afraid my little legs started shaking. I stood in panic as the dogs approached the gate. I noticed the gate had come back in place as if it was closed and locked. The dogs ran up to the gate and suddenly stopped running. All they needed to do was tap the gate with their noses, and they would have discovered the gate was broken and open. But the way they stood there was weird. They did not attempt to go any further. It was as if someone was standing in front of the gate and stopping them from approaching it. All of a sudden, a man came out of his home across the street from where I was standing. He yelled at the dogs to scatter or run away. He threw a large rock at them, and they started to scatter. I believe in my heart God closed the gate and an angel stood at it.

"The LORD shall cause thine enemies that rise up against thee to be smitten before thy face: they shall come out against thee one way, and flee before thee seven ways" (Deuteronomy 28:7).

Childhood Testimonies (Give Me a Quarter, Please?)

When I was a child, I had nine other siblings, making it very unlikely for our father to give all of us allowances. My dad was the only one working in our large family. He was a local truck driver, so having money for candy was a luxury. There was a candy store around the corner where I lived. They had the best-tasting pecan cookies I ever tasted. I wanted so badly to go to that candy store that I used to ask total strangers walking down the street for a dime. One day, my mother caught me asking, and she promised if she ever heard me asking another stranger for money, she would give me a spanking I would never forget. Well, that completely stopped me on track. I think God allowed me to get caught to protect me and also for me to get to know Him.

One day, I was walking down the street with nothing to do but think about candy. I looked up to the sky and said, "God, can You give me a quarter, please?" I thought He was big enough for me to ask Him for a quarter instead of a dime. As I continued to walk, I saw something very colorful in the middle of the sidewalk. As I approached it, I discovered it was a small colorful beaded coin purse with a zipper. I looked around to see if anyone was looking and quickly picked it up. I opened it, and to my surprise, it was loaded with quarters, dimes, and nickels. There is no doubt in my mind that God placed it there just for me. Amazingly, it was right in front of a candy store. I felt as if I found a secret friend: God.

> For everyone who asks receives; he who seeks finds; and to him who knocks, the door will be opened. Which of you, if his son asks for

bread, will give him a stone? Or if he asks for a fish, will give him a snake? If you, then, though you are evil, know how to give good gifts to your children, how much more will your Father in heaven give good gifts to those who ask him!

Matthew 7:8-11 (NIV)

Exercising Your Memory

Think about your relationship with God as a child. Can you write a childhood testimony?

_____

_____

_____

_____

_____

_____

_____

_____

_____

_____

_____

_____

_____

Imagination Comes from God

During my childhood, my bad memories outnumbered the good ones: There were many times I wanted so badly to be alone to meditate on things that happened, but often I would get interrupted by one of my siblings. Daydreaming on an optimistic level was a way for me to escape. I daydreamed incessantly, not only to escape from the bad memories, but I also had a very creative mind. (I read that daydreaming helps children process information and explore ideas.) If I looked at pictures in magazines, books, or a picture hanging on a wall, I could create in my mind an entire story from the picture.

At times, daydreaming got me into trouble, especially when I would daydream in school. I flunked the fifth grade because of it. I was not in class mentally, though I was sitting in the class physically. I often took trips and adventures with wonderful thoughts. I did not understand that having a vivid, colorful imagination is a gift from God, which is a blessing for writers. When you are able to see what you're writing, you're helping the readers make a picture they can relate to. The writer has a clearer vision and guidance.

The devil starts early in a child's mind to destroy the good thoughts and transform them into bad ones. As adults, we have control of what we think about. Oftentimes, while writing, you may receive a negative thought about what you wrote, which may cause you to rip it up or toss it away. Please never toss or rip up your work. If you feel you do not like it, hang on to it anyway. Find a place to file all the work you decided to stop writing or simply don't think it was good enough.

I once crumpled up a poem but decided not to throw it away. I unwrinkled it and filed it away. One day while visiting an uncle in New York, I met an illustrator of children's books who asked me to write a child's poem about Christmas. I thought I could not write children's poems until I remembered the poem I almost threw away. The illustrator loved it, but his publishers would not allow him to use it. The simple fact that he loved it helped me know it was not so bad after all. Please take note: If you have spent time writing something and all of a sudden you don't like it, do not react too quickly by tossing it. File it away and come back to it another time. Oftentimes, you will find that you like it and have a desire to complete what you started. The poem was titled "A Crystal Holiday," which inspired me to write another child's poem, titled "Fluffy Confetti."

A Crystal Holiday

A little girl with short nappy curls,
Small button brown eyes, full of mystery and surprise.
Company, there were plenty—the middle child of many.
Five older and four younger siblings she had,
She never sought leadership like the first;
She had no desire to follow like the last.
She was a diamond in the rough, waiting for the dark clouds to pass.
A dreamer she was, her escape to get away
From all the hustle and bustle of a very confusing day.
Deep thinking gave her the flexibility to flee from reality,
To walk into her fantasy of a "crystal holiday":
Aluminum gold, emerald green, candy apple red,
Shiny and new sparkling silver shingles that jingle,
"Merry Christmas to you."
The smell of popcorn strings intertwines with the wood of a freshly cut pine.
On the tip of the top were the eyes of an angel watching

over me.
What's inside lovely wrapped packages tied
with ribbons and bows?
Who knows, but could it? Would it be?
A gift-wrapped so beautifully just for me!
I wonder what was under the tree, anxious to see,
So I decided I would just enjoy and wait patiently.
Candied berries with momma's old-fashioned labels on
a table,
Antique beige lace with a chocolate cake and sweet
potato pies
Between two candles reflecting the fire in her eyes.
A fireplace with the sound of crackling wood feeling
perfectly right,
the comforts of a rocking chair with music
in the air, the visions of a silent night.
Sounds of pots and pans from a busy kitchen.
Not to mention the aroma of yeast rising bread,
All the mixings and fixings send a smell to her head.
No mistaking what was baking, and soon we'll be fed.
A stuffed turkey full of cornbread dressing season for
Teasing,
An aroma that was absolutely pleasing
From the top of a hot stove to the hanging of mistletoe.
Pressing against a cold windowpane, freezing her
nose,

Looking out, searching for the falling of fluffy white
snow,
Then a vision of flakes glistening under a moonlight
glow.
Her joy was ascending,
But she knew the thoughts were ending of her "crystal
holiday"
When she heard her brother screaming,
"There she goes again—dreaming!"

The Snowy Testimony

We all know Chicago is very unpredictable when it comes to the weather. I have lived alone for five years since my daughter got married. I live just outside of Chicago in the western suburbs area. Sharon and I used to shovel snow together, and I started to realize another set of hands should never be taken for granted. The first winter after her wedding, we had a big downfall of snow. I came home from work around 8:30 p.m. Not only did I come home late because my job at that time was very busy, but I also needed to stop at a store and get salt for the snow. I had no idea it had snowed so much while I was at work. I worked inside a cubicle, and there was no window nearby to look out of.

I heard from my coworkers it was snowing, but I did not have time to get up to look out. I continued working, and by the end of the day, when I walked out to go home, I was in shock. I could not believe it had snowed that much. I was tired and did not feel like taking all the snow off my car, let alone shoveling snow when I got home. After taking all the snow off my car, I stopped at the store for the salt and finally made it home.

I ate dinner, and that made me very sleepy. I usually pray after dinner when I come in from work. I came in late, and I worried a bit about the time. I knew if I waited until morning, I might be late for work. I was not sure what to do. I decided I would pray first in spite of the snow or how late it might be. I needed help from God, so I asked Him for it while praying. I said, "Lord, You said You would be my husband. I really need Your strength now. Can You help me with the snow?" I did not know what He was going to do, but I took that one shovel and said, "Lord, it's You and me now."

I had a large driveway, the front walkway, my front steps, the back near my garage, and my back steps to shovel. It looked like miles and hills of snow. I started to think about the Lord, and He gave me strength. He took my mind off shoveling snow even though my body kept on working.

All I remember after I was nearly finished was looking up and not believing I was almost finished. When I finished, I still had so much energy that I took on the dishes in my sink and even cleaned my house a little. I was on a roll! Joy filled my soul, and I began to praise Him. I never felt such a boost of energy before after a hard day at work like I had that day. It was then that I realized what it meant when He said, "Your Maker is your husband."

I have been calling on Him ever since that day, and He has never let me down. He is truly my husband, my king, and I love Him.

"For thy Maker is thine husband; the LORD of hosts is his name; and thy redeemer the Holy One of Israel; The God of the whole earth shall he be called" (Isaiah 54:5).

Fluffy Confetti

Flakes of snow on a winter day know exactly what to do,
Fluffy confetti falling steady and sticking like crazy glue,
Floating to the ground without a sound during a quiet, silent night.
When anxious eyes awake, surprised to see the darkness
has turned snow-white,
Delivered from above with a touch of love, like flowers on a summer day,
It floats in mid-air, bringing joy to share on a Christmas holiday.
On mountaintops, it gently drops softly and gracefully,

Filling the ground without a sound for sparkling eyes
to see.
A bundle of cold sun just making fun for a child like a
favorite toy,
When winter sings a song, it brings happiness, peace,
and joy.
Fluffy confetti prepared and ready to be tossed for fun
and play,
And after its season, without a reason, it just lies down
and
melts away.

The "I Am" Experience

My desire to know God's power and His character started to develop in me when I started listening to a particular minister on television during the early stages of my new salvation. This minister was the very first pastor who taught the Bible in a way where I could fully understand it. My eyes of understanding were also opened when the hands of God touched me. I was so inspired to learn about Jesus that I purchased many of his books and CDs. Whenever anyone let me know they had his teaching, I would borrow it and later purchase it. I still have many of them today.

One day while listening to him on TV, my desire to tell others about Christ was overwhelming. I stopped watching for a moment to pray. "Oh God, could You teach me to speak like this minister? If I could only describe You the way he does, I would tell the entire world about how awesome You are."

Suddenly, a question popped into my mind: "Who do you say that I am?" At that time, I had no idea this question was asked of Peter in the Bible. I was a new Christian, and there were many chapters in the Bible I had not read yet.

The question repeated in my head again: "Who does Lena say that I am?" I got a pen and paper and started to write line by line who I thought the Lord was.

My first thoughts were, *You were here before clocks,* so I wrote a line, "You were before clocks ticked time." I kept writing until all the lines started to develop into a poem called "I Am."

Later during the week, I went to the midweek service at my church. I had only been going there for a few months. I was well acquainted with the pastor because I met him prior to attending the church by making an appointment to meet him. After meeting him, it was confirmed this was the church I was supposed to attend. The midweek service started, and I sat in the first row. I will never forget when the pastor started to read the passage in Exodus when God asked Moses to tell Pharaoh to let His people go. Then Moses asked God, "Who shall I say sent me?" And God said, "'I Am has sent you unto them."

At that moment, my eyes were opened, and I was so surprised that this passage was in the Bible.

I thought the question God asked me was only my thoughts. But God was explaining to me, "It is not who the minister on TV says I am, but who am I to you?" I realized my experience with God had to be personal. Revelation filled me until tears started to flow. My pastor noticed the surprised expression on my face. He stopped speaking at that moment and asked me if I had something to say. I was embarrassed, but I told him that I had written a poem much like his sermon. He then asked if I would recite it. I got up and recited the poem I wrote about God, "I Am." Not only had God made my wish come true by allowing me to tell others about Him, but He also gave me a powerful revelation.

It's not about what others know about God; it's about our personal relationship with Him because when we seek Him, we will find Him, and He wants us to know Him personally. This is called a personal relationship because God wants each of us to tell others about our individual experiences with Him, much like He did with Peter.

"But what about you?" he asked. "Who do you say I am?" Simon Peter answered, "You are the Christ, the Son of the living God." Jesus replied, "Blessed are you, Simon son of Jonah, for this was not revealed to you by man, but by my Father in heaven."

Matthew 16:15-17 (NIV)

My thoughts about God are my personal thoughts developed through an intimate relationship with Him. Many years after I wrote "I Am," I began to trust Him through my storms and got to know His marvelous love for me. Trusting Him and discovering His power over the storms in my life produced a reverence for Him. I began to hate sin because sin is what separates us from His presence when we do not repent. I realized more and more how much I needed Him, how much I loved Him, how much He loved me. I had mind-blowing experiences that increased my spiritual development and intimacy with God. Prayer became more natural and was not confined to a church or a particular time. I pray whenever He comes to my mind, and that is quite often now. "I Am" means: I can be whatever I need to be: a father, mother, doctor, provider, teacher, lover, friend, way maker, protector. Nothing is impossible with the Great I Am. Who is He to you?

Who is God to You?

In the space below, write down your thoughts about God. Please do not write down what you have heard about Him. I want you to think about your personal experiences. Make it personal.

Moses said to God, "Suppose I go to the Israelites and say to them, 'The God of your fathers
has sent me to you,' and they ask me, 'What is
his name?' Then what shall I tell them?" God
said to Moses, "I AM WHO I AM. This is what
you are to say to the Israelites: 'I AM has sent
me to you.'" God also said to Moses, "Say to
the Israelites, 'The LORD, the God of your fathers—the God of Abraham, the God of Isaac
and the God of Jacob—has sent me to you.'
This is my name forever, the name by which
I am to be remembered from generation to
generation."

Exodus 3:13-15 (NIV)

I Am

I am before clocks ticked time.
I am the peace within the mind.
I am human in personality.
I am life in reality.
I am the beam in light.
I turn wrong to right.
I am Alpha and Omega.
I am love; I am the Creator.
I live in supreme.
I am light well seen.
I am absolute in truth.

I put young in youth.
I am strength in food.
I put win in lose.
I am fly in the wing.
I am song in sing.
I am growth; I am a seed.
I am the everlasting need.
I am a teacher; I am college.
I am reason; I am knowledge.
I am a helmet for salvation.
I am design for all nations.
I am the maker of color.
I am Lord of father and mother.
I am the hand that created man.
I am the Rock on which he stands.
I am absolute; I am whole.
I am power; I control.
I am fight.
I am shield. I am my word; I am will.
I am the spirit in living.
I am the reason for giving.
I am love in your heart.
I put together in apart.
I am the maker of all seasons.
I am why for all reasons.
I am He that is, was, and is to come.
Besides Me, there is no one.
I Am God!

The Late Walk
Under the Viaduct

My daughter Sharon and I lived together for a number of years before she got married. We lived on the north side of Chicago and would often take late walks to get in a little exercise before retiring to bed. The walks would also give us the privilege to bond as mother and daughter. We walked for at least three miles every other night. My daughter was saved not long after my salvation, and we were growing spiritually together for Christ as we enjoyed each other's company. We would never miss out on any given opportunity to minister to people about the goodness of the Lord. There were many occasions people would give their heart to the Lord after we ministered to them. We went home smiling because God gave us this awesome privilege.

One night, we took our walk a little later than usual; it was around 11:00 p.m. We walked down the street of Devon Avenue. As we headed toward a viaduct, we noticed a lady around fifty or sixty years old, sitting in a chair with a grocery cart nearby. Inside the cart were her personal belongings. We thought she did not have the appearance of a typical homeless person. She had a very neat, clean personal appearance. We decided to approach her to talk with her and maybe minister to her. We asked her how she became homeless, and she explained to us how she lost her job. We decided to give her some money so she could get something to eat because she informed us that she was also hungry. After blessing her with a little cash, we were about to pray for her when out of nowhere, a two-door black truck drove by with a strange-looking bald-headed man hanging out of the window, screaming at us as if he was angry. He told us to leave the lady alone. We thought this guy had to be crazy, and we continued to talk to the lady because we thought he had left. We did not expect him to return, but shortly after that rude episode, he came back and this time angrier than before.

He circled the block, immediately parked his truck, and jumped out, screaming profanity. The window was let down on the driver's side of the truck. He leaned over the window and pulled something out that appeared to be a knife or maybe a gun. He pushed it inside his jacket pocket and started running toward my daughter and me. He was screaming profanity and making threats to kill us. This incident was happening so fast, my daughter and I could only stand in shock and fear. As he quickly approached us, he yelled out in this horrifying voice, "I am going to cut your tongues out and make you eat them!" My daughter and I looked at each other, confused and shocked. We did not have a chance to run because he would have surely caught us.

I believe he also wanted us to run, but something in both of us would not allow us to. The homeless lady in the chair was also surprised and shocked. My daughter immediately started praying, speaking in tongues, and I looked up to the sky. I said to God, "God, I know You are not going to let this guy kill us!" When he ran over to us, words came out of my mouth like a sharp-edged sword. I looked directly into his eyes and said, "No weapon formed against us will prosper!"

Suddenly he stopped and calmed down and looked very puzzled as if something completely took over him. He started to apologize and even made a bizarre statement. He said, "I like black people, I have black friends." As crazy as this story sounds, my daughter and I suddenly felt peace. The peace was more powerful than the fear. We explained to him we were getting ready to pray for this lady. Believe it or not, he joined us in prayer. After the prayer, we walked away, knowing that something very powerful just happened that night. God had just done something we had never seen before. As we walked away, this man that appeared to be very scary and dangerous was continuing to apologize. He stood in the same place, apologizing until we walked out of his sight.

My daughter, Sharon, looked at me and said, "Ma, the Word works! Oh my God, it works! The words came from your mouth like a sword! I can't believe it." I was so happy, and at the same time, I felt stronger and bold. I told my daughter, "For sure, it works!" Our walk even changed. We started to walk with confidence.

After we got home, I could not sleep right away; I only looked up at the ceiling, thanking God and thinking about what had just transpired. God replied to me, saying, "I only wanted you to know what was in you."

> No weapon that is formed against thee shall prosper; and every tongue that shall rise against thee in judgment thou shalt condemn. This is the heritage of the servants of the LORD, and their righteousness is of me, saith the LORD.
>
> Isaiah 54:17

Praying for a House

My daughter and I were so silly when we first started out as new believers. We thought whatever we asked for, even if it belonged to someone else, we were determined to get. One day, we drove by a beautiful house in the city of Chicago because we were looking for a home. We got out of our car and prayed in front of the house. People were still occupying the house, and it was a very large one. We bound the devil for someone else's home. We said, "That is our house, and the people who live here have to move in the name of Jesus."

We currently lived in a small condo with one bedroom. It was a nice condo, but we had no way to look out of the windows. All the windows faced a large brick building. I love rain, and every time it rained, I could only hear it but never see it. In between the buildings were more pigeons than one could imagine. All they would do was poop on my windowsills and make a lot of noise. Whenever they were mating, the noise was unbearable. At times, some of the tenants who lived in the building would allow their dogs to roam free while they were still in their apartments, preparing to go out. Needless to say, my daughter and I had a strong desire to have a house of our own. I wanted windows and a front and back porch.

I put my condo up for sale. The ad appeared in the newspapers and websites for two years. Only one couple came to look at it, and they never called us back. I eventually took it off the market and decided to wait for God. One day while attending the midweek service at our local church, the pastor prophesied that it was time for someone to buy a house. I knew it was God telling me to put my condo up for sale and go house hunting ASAP. I heard a word from God that not only touched my ears but also touched my heart. I called my real estate agent the next day. I told her to put the condo back up for sale.

Lo and behold, we got a buyer for the condo the next week. I found a house the following week. Everything was going quickly. I had enough for a down payment because God gave me wisdom on how to refinance my condo and pay off all my debt one year prior to our interest in purchasing a home. After He gave me instructions to refinance, He told me to put the money in the bank and not to touch it. I did exactly that. Even though my daughter needed money for school and I wanted badly to help her, God told me to allow her to trust Him as well. That's another testimony because she did, and I will let you in on the details later.

Getting back to the purchase of the house: My daughter, the real estate agent, and I went looking for a home one week after we got a buyer for the condo. We came to a home that my daughter was totally against buying because she had a very bad feeling about the area. I was so excited; I never even noticed the area. God confirmed her feelings when we had trouble opening the door. The real estate agent tried, and she was unsuccessful. She called the owner, and he, too, had trouble opening the door. I finally concluded this was a bad sign, and we decided against looking at this house. The owner later told us he had a home he was rehabbing, and even though it was not ready, he wanted us to see it. It was only a few blocks away. Once we arrived at the home that was being rehabbed, I walked into the kitchen, and the Lord said to me, "This is your home." I was excited and started to cry. We signed the contract, got back into the car to head home when my daughter said she had heard from the Lord prior to our arrival at the house. She said she wanted to tell me when we were alone.

My daughter was still attending cooking school, so I had to take care of the business deals by myself. I had to get a closing lawyer. I learned a lot through this process. Finally, on closing day, I had run completely out of money. With the down payment and everything else that goes along with purchasing a home, I ran out of money very quickly. I was also told I needed to bring a check of $1,500 more at the closing. The $1,500 was the last of my savings. I started to worry. We purchased the home without a washer, dryer, stove, and refrigerator because the home was newly rehabbed, and the price was dropped substantially because of it. Yet, I was completely broke. I felt as if I was stuck between a rock and a hard place. I took my Bible with me to the closing. I made it there before everyone else. I started to read my Bible and pray.

"Oh God, I don't trust anyone but You. I don't know how I am going to pay my first mortgage, not to mention the stove and refrigerator I had to purchase. Please, Lord, I trust You alone." Everyone came after I had my talk with the Lord. We all sat at a long table in a conference room in the closing office. The buyer and his lawyer sat across the table from my lawyer and me. Just before the closing ended, the buyer's lawyer looked across the table at my lawyer's documents. It appeared she was being a little nosey. Suddenly, she asked my lawyer if he would step outside the room. When they both came back into the room, the buyer's lawyer informed me that I had a $7,000 check, and they gave it to me right at that moment.

All I know is I came in expecting to give them $1,500, but I left the closing with not only the same $1,500 I came with but an additional $7,000. As I walked away to my car, my mind could not receive what just happened.

But my heart was filled with the joy of knowing God answered my prayer. Oh boy, did He answer my prayer!

"And God is able to make all grace abound toward you; that ye, always having all sufficiency in all things, may abound to every good work" (2 Corinthians 9:8).

God is Involved in Every Detail of Our Lives

When my daughter and I moved into our new home, we were tired. We had packed most of the night and spent the next morning putting things in order for the movers. After the movers left, we were exhausted and sleepy. We looked at all the windows and felt as if the entire world were watching us from the outside. There were no shades or blinds on the windows. It looked like a glasshouse.

God truly answered my prayers. We had a home with twenty-eight windows. When I prayed for a home, I asked the Lord for many windows. I love rain and thunder, and I wanted to see rain fall. My last place of residence had windows, but the view was a large brick wall. My apartment faced another building. The house was newly rehabbed, and the owner did not consider the windows. Even though we were tired, we headed off to a hardware store, rushing before closing. We measured all the windows and had to purchase blinds for twenty-eight windows. We quickly came home and tried to put them up. Neither my daughter nor I had ever attempted to put up blinds. I thought it was simple as one-two-three, but trying to hammer a nail in wood for the blinds was like trying to put a nail in brick.

We could not understand why the wood was so hard. Not only were our arms tired, but it also took nearly the entire day to move all our furniture. We were exhausted and frustrated and began to get upset with each other. I remember the voice of God came to my head: "Cover the windows with sheets and go to bed." My daughter insisted on trying to put up the blinds, and I wanted to obey the voice in my head by putting sheets on the windows until morning and go directly to bed.

My daughter thought it would be very embarrassing to put bed sheets on the windows. I tried explaining to my daughter that God wanted us to get some rest, but she refused to quit. She continued trying until she could not hold her arms up. Finally, she gave up, we prayed, and both went to bed. Early morning the next day, I had a vivid vision before completely waking up. I saw hands putting up blinds. I saw metal behind the wood on the windows. The windows were made of storm wood and metal. I heard the word "drill bits," but I misunderstood and thought I heard "drill bites." For the few of those who, like myself, never put up blinds or never did handy work, let me explain what drill bits are: They can be purchased for simple manual drilling by hand or for a power drill. Power drilling is needed for very hard surfaces like metal. I saw in my vision a hand holding a power drill. Believe it or not, I had a small power drill, and I cannot remember where or when I got it. It was probably a gift. Needless to say, it was never used until then. I suddenly woke up and knew exactly what to do.

I told my daughter, "I know now what to do. We need to go to the hardware store and get some drill bites." I used the wrong term, and when we arrived at the hardware store, I asked an employee who helped customers look for materials, "Where would I find drill bites?" Looking very confused, he replied, "Who?" I replied, "You know! Drill bites." He said, "Do you mean drill bits?" I said, "Yes, drill bits." I did not care what he was thinking about me. At least I was in the ballpark. We finally got what we needed, and we came home and put up twenty-six blinds in one day. God taught me how to put up blinds.

It may seem like a small job, but it was a big deal to my daughter and me. It was also a big deal to God, who understood our need. He understood our frustration. There are no problems too small or too large for our

God. He was touched by the feeling of our infirmities and became a present help in the time of need.

"In the day of my trouble I will call upon thee: for thou wilt answer me" (Psalm 86:7).

"I called upon the LORD in distress: the LORD answered me, and set me in a large place" (Psalm 118:5).

Small Problem with Big Frustration

Has there ever been a problem that appeared to be small, but it carried big frustration? Did the Lord solve a small problem that most people would have thought of as nothing, but God understood and solved the problem?

Please use the space below to explain.

_____

_____

_____

_____

_____

_____

_____

_____

_____

My Brother Larry's Toe

My brother Larry came to stay with me for a while. I gave him one of my bedrooms on the second floor of my home. He would often walk around upstairs without shoes because of the carpet. One early Saturday morning, he was getting ready to go off to work. I was sitting down, watching television, when I suddenly heard a loud thumping sound, like the sounds at the bowling alley. I heard my brother yell out very loudly, "My toe! I broke my toe!"

I looked around and realized he had actually fallen down the stairs that led to the upstairs bedroom. Somehow, while falling or after his fall, he landed on his second toe on his right foot. The toe was completely bent into an "L" shape and was lying across his big toe. He was screaming and cursing so loudly I could not really understand what happened. Needless to say, he was in a lot of pain. I quickly called 911, then tried to calm him down. I asked him to sit on the couch.

He hopped over to the couch as he continued to yell out in pain. I was hoping for the ambulance to come quickly when I suddenly received a tug on my spirit from God.

He said to me, "Lay your hands on your brother's toe, and I will heal him." I asked my brother to calm down so that I could pray for him. He finally started to calm down, and I was able to place my hand on his toe and pray. I prayed for a few minutes. When I had completed the prayer, my brother started to look and act calmer than before. He looked at me as if everything might be okay.

Then he reached down and put his toe back in place. I looked at him and said, "You are healed. Get up and walk." He got up from the couch and started to walk, and we started to praise God. A few minutes later, the ambulance was ringing my front doorbell. After opening the door, I explained to them that my brother was healed, but they could check him out so that he could have confirmation. They came over to him asked him what happened. While he was explaining to them how he fell down a flight of stairs, one of the paramedics examined his right foot, looking at the toe that was supposed to have been broken. They got up and proclaimed his toe was fine and it did not look broken at all.

My brother and I both saw how his toe was out of line.

We both knew that God healed him.

We are given the power to heal, but we must believe. When God waves the flag for healing, we must act in faith and believe, and nothing will be impossible.

"But he was wounded for our transgressions, he was bruised for our iniquities: the chastisement of our peace was upon him; and with his stripes we are healed" (Isaiah 53:5).

"Behold, I give unto you power to tread on serpents and scorpions, and over all the power of the enemy: and nothing shall by any means hurt you" (Luke 10:9).

About the Author

Lena Edwards is an anointed inspirational writer, speaker, and teacher. God has given her an exceptional ability to write in many different forms: poetry, plays, children's books, magazine articles, and songs. Lena has written over a hundred inspiring poems, including several songs, as well as written and produced plays.

Her life, like many others, was on a continuous downward spiral, filled with many heartaches and pain. In 1999, she gave her heart to the Lord. After that day, her life moved to an upward spiral. Yes, like everyone else, she still faces storms, even as a Christian. She is now experiencing joy like she had never before. The big difference from the storms in her life prior to 1999 is that now she found a safe haven with the Lord. She does not regret the stormy experiences in her life because they have led her to the Lord, the God who is her prince of peace. The power of God has not only helped her through the storms of life but has put up roadblocks to keep them from harming her.

Lena's trials have turned into triumphs because of the love of God. As a Christian, she has accomplished goals that she thought she could never accomplish before her salvation. Each test in Lena's life has led to eye-opening testimonies that are shared in her book. Many of the testimonies she shared with others have led them to Christ. She loves the Lord, so it is easy for her to talk about His goodness and grace in her life. Her book, Spiritual Rose, is filled with many personal testimonies.

Through much hard work and determination, she has emerged to become a powerful spiritual writing teacher, inspirational speaker, and writer. Within the rhythm of Lena's poetry and teaching and the elegance of her presentations is her unique ability to captivate audiences from all walks of life. This book will increase your faith as it builds your belief in God. It will help you get started writing your story or verbally telling others your testimony of how God has helped you make it through life. We all need the Lord desperately. Let's share our stories as we glorify the Lord because there are many people who need to hear them.

Because of her love for writing, she has a program titled "Inspirational Ink" that encourages and inspires through the art of creative writing. She has taught several classes on creative writing, writing as a form for self-healing so that others will believe in the Lord and be encouraged.

For speaking engagements, please reach out to lena_edwards@sbcglobal.net or text at 630-235-3539.